D1261533

The Complete Home Guide
to Making Pillows, Draperies, Lampshades, Quilts, and Slipcovers.

The Complete Home Guide
to Making Pillows, Draperies, Lampshades, Quilts, and Slipcovers.

Angela Fishburn

Larousse and Co., Inc *New York*

For my Mother

© Angela Fishburn 1978
First published 1978 in the United States
by Larousse & Co., Inc.
572 Fifth Avenue
New York. N.Y. 10036
ISBN 0–88332–090–8
Library of Congress Catalog Card Number 78–54046
Printed in Great Britain
Second Printing 1979

Contents

Acknowledgment

The author and publishers wish to thank
A Sanderson & Son Ltd for permission to
reproduce colour illustrations 1 and 2, and
also Mark Gerson for photographing colour
illustrations 3, 4, 5, 6 and the illustrations
which appear on the jacket.

AUTHOR'S NOTE

All the measurements in this book are given
in metric units followed by imperial units
in brackets. The conversions are in many
cases only approximate, and the reader
should use only one of these two systems
consistently throughout the book.

Introduction

Soft furnishings play such an important part in all our homes that it is well worth spending time and trouble on their planning and construction.

Making your own soft furnishings is one of the most rewarding aspects of needlework. Few things are more satisfactory than creating practical and attractive things for the home, at prices you can afford. A great deal of money can be saved by mastering the processes and techniques explained in this book, and I feel sure that you will be well rewarded for your time and effort.

Do our homes reflect our personalities? Is your home bright and stimulating or quiet and restful? A home should be a pleasant relaxing place in which to live with our families and entertain our friends. This can often be achieved by using imaginative and original ideas for making successful colour schemes and soft furnishings. Try to develop an awareness of colour, design and texture; above all — enjoy making and choosing a background for yourself and your family, which will reflect your personality and be original in concept.

This book is intended particularly for those who enjoy creating, and who have a basic knowledge of needlework. I hope too, that it will serve as a guide and inspiration to the beginner, enabling her to progress with confidence from making small items to those that demand perhaps a little more skill.

1· Colour, Design and Texture

Developing a decorating scheme and making the soft furnishings — experimenting with colour, texture and fabric, to discover harmony or contrast — can bring a great sense of achievement when the room is successfully completed.

Try to achieve the maximum effect with the least expense. Remember that costly fabrics do not necessarily provide the most interesting schemes. Look at the less expensive fabrics and see how, with a little imagination, they can be used to advantage. Interior designers sometimes use the most unexpected materials to create the most exciting effects.

Before embarking on the processes and techniques of making soft furnishings for the home, it is useful to consider a little of what is involved in making a successful decorative scheme: for this is the basis of success.

Colour, design and texture are the three considerations to take into account, and in order to understand something of how these work together, it is important to study each separately before attempting to combine them.

COLOUR

The Oxford Dictionary defines colour as 'the sensation produced in the eye by rays of decomposed light'. Colour, therefore, is only present when there is light. The colour of an object seen in sunlight is different from that seen in candlelight, because the intensity of the light being reflected from the object's surface is different, and therefore the colour seems to vary.

Colour is also influenced by its surroundings, and can take on an entirely fresh tone when accompanied by different colours and textures.

The colour wheel
The colour wheel is the starting point in planning a decorative scheme and is often called 'nature's rainbow'. Make a colour wheel, and experiment with paper and paint to see how it works. Notice how the wheel is divided into two: one half provides the warm colours — reds, oranges and yellows — and the other half the cool colours — greens, blues and purples (fig. 1).

The principles of colour
Primary colours
There are three primary colours — red, yellow and blue. These are the three basic constituents of the colour spectrum.
Secondary colours
These secondary colours are produced by mixing two of the adjoining primary colours together: orange (made by mixing red and yellow), green (made by mixing blue and yellow) and purple (made by mixing blue and red). An infinite number of colours can be obtained by mixing these secondary colours.

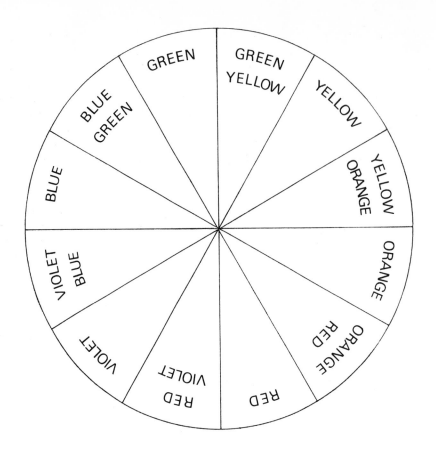

Fig. 1 **Colour wheel**

Neutrals

In addition to the primary and secondary colours there are two neutrals — black and white. White reflects the light and absorbs other colours around it. Black absorbs the light and intensifies the colours around it and so makes things look brighter. Black and white are the extremes of the neutrals, but there are also greys and browns. These vary considerably and can create warmth or coolness. A grey/blue, for example, would be cooler than a grey/yellow. This also applies to browns, an orange/brown being warmer than a blue/brown.

Hue

A hue is colour in its purest form.

Tone

Tone is the darkening or lightening of these pure colours.

Colour value

This is the ability of a colour to reflect light.

Harmony

The colours that are adjacent to each other in the colour circle are known to be 'harmonious', or 'in harmony' with each other: for example, green, blue/green, blue.

Complementary

Complementary colours lie opposite to one another in the colour circle and are in contrast to each other: for example, red/green.

Discordant

These are colours that are out of their natural order and are conflicting. They are neither in harmony, nor complementary to each other. They do not coexist well and can create an inharmonious combination.

Some points to bear in mind when using colour

(1) Try to understand as much as possible about colour and how it works (see the Bibliography at the end of this book). Then use it with confidence and flair. Do not be afraid of it.

(2) A colour or hue is influenced by the one that adjoins it, and it appears lighter or darker depending on that influence. Experiment with colours, putting one against the other, and giving them different backgrounds; notice how the colours change when doing this. Using paper and paint, or scraps of fabric, see how many different effects can be achieved.

(3) Always look at wallpapers, fabrics, etc., in both artificial light and daylight.

(4) The tone of the colours (the degree of lightness and darkness) changes with the gradual movement of the sun throughout the day. Therefore a room and its furnishings will appear different with the variations in intensity of light from dawn to dusk each day. It will also be affected by the amount and type of artificial light provided by lamps and bulbs.

(5) Colour creates illusions of shape and size; hence the ability to make a room look larger or smaller, narrower or wider. Remember, too, that a colour appears brighter when used in large areas.

DESIGN

The size, shape and layout of a room should be complemented and enhanced by the patterns and visual shapes created by the fabrics.

(1) In order to train the eye to appreciate good design, look carefully at film, television and theatre sets, glossy magazines, window displays, fashion displays and expensive couture clothes. All the designers responsible for these have a trained appreciation of pattern and shape, and much can be learned from studying their work.

(2) Too much pattern in a room is ineffectual. It gives a cluttered look and makes the room appear too busy. Pattern should be used skilfully, taking balance and contrast into account.

(3) Use small or geometric patterns in small rooms and keep large patterns for large rooms. Very large patterns are more suited to public buildings and hotels.

(4) Horizontal or diagonal stripes should be used cautiously, as these can clash with other patterns in a room. They can, however, be used effectively if matching in tone with other furnishings. For example, try using stripes for a roller blind, or a pair of curtains, against a background of patterned wallpaper. Horizontal stripes lengthen the wall, vertical stripes shorten it or reduce the length.

(5) Above all, the fabric chosen should suit its purpose and be functional, and at the same time should be decorative.

TEXTURE

Texture adds yet another dimension to the decorating scheme. Take into account the area of wood-block floor, brick wall, or pieces of polished furniture. These must all be considered for the texture and colour they provide.

Textures can add interest to a room without the need for colour. Natural surfaces such as wood, brick, rush matting or knobbly tweed can be the perfect background for a successful scheme.

Contrast in texture is as important as contrast in colour. Texture affects the value of colour. For instance a coloured article which has a rough-textured object placed next to it will look quite different when placed beside a smooth or shiny-surfaced object. This is because the shiny object reflects the light, while the rough object absorbs it.

Variations in texture give a room interest. In order to appreciate the value of texture, try collecting as many fabrics as possible in one colour but in different textures.

THE DECORATING SCHEME

To make a successful scheme, it is necessary to look at the picture as a whole and not to be tempted to consider each item in isolation. Plan carefully using a notebook and pencil. If possible make a sketch of the room, noting electrical points, elevations and existing furniture. Collect samples of fabrics, wallpapers and paints. Keep a folder for each room scheme and be businesslike. Take along the folder when looking for samples.

Try to create a scheme that you will not tire of quickly and that suits both the aspect of the room and its purpose. First choose the basic or main colour, and then work round it. There are three types of scheme that work well.

Monochromatic
This is a scheme using different tones and amounts of one colour. This can be most effective if care is given to balance and pattern, and interest created by variations in texture. Too much of the same tone can be dull, so use some bright accessories.

Related
This uses colours that are adjoining on the colour wheel. Use of these related colours creates a restful, harmonious scheme (e.g. blues/greens).

Contrasting
A contrasting, or complementary, scheme is one which uses two colours that are opposite to one another on the colour wheel. It is often advisable, however, to let one colour dominate as this creates a more interesting scheme; then use a vibrant colour to give emphasis to a particular focal point (e.g. yellow/violet).

Planning a successful scheme
There are many points that must be remembered when planning a decorating scheme:

(1) Consider the aspect of the room. North- and east-facing rooms demand warm colour schemes to counteract the lack of sunshine and low intensity of light. Base the scheme on the warmer tones of reds, oranges or yellows.

(2) Rooms that face south and west have strong sunlight streaming in during the day. They can take the cool fresh colours of blues and greens.

(3) Decide on a basic colour which is pleasing to those who use the room most. Ideally, the carpet should be chosen first, the wall colour next, and then the curtains. These represent the three largest areas of colour in the room and will therefore have the most impact, so they must work well together.

(4) If planning from scratch, consider having the same basic colour throughout the house; or certainly make sure that adjoining carpets are in harmony with each other. This creates a great sense of spaciousness and continuity, and avoids the 'bits-and-pieces' look. It enables room schemes to be built round a common colour. Separate schemes must, of course, be made for each room; by using varying amounts of colour, texture and pattern, a pleasing overall effect can then be achieved. Take care when choosing a carpet and make sure that it will work well with many colours.

(5) Collect samples of fabrics suitable for the main items of soft furnishings, e.g. curtains, loose covers, upholstery. Use complementary colours for the accessories such as cushions and lampshades.

(6) Remember that by grouping accessories together, whether they are cushions or ornaments, they have more impact.

(7) Do not always opt for safety by creating a monochromatic scheme. Make a room come to life by adding startling touches

of contrasting or complementary colours. For example, when using yellow as a basic colour, the accessory colours could be orange, pink or bright green.

(8) Distribute the colours around the room so that the overall effect satisfies the eye and is well-balanced. Too much pattern on one side of the room can create an unbalanced effect. Experiment by placing furniture in different positions to achieve a good balance, and, if possible, group furniture to take advantage of sunlight. Try putting a plain chair near to patterned curtains, or vice versa. If making loose covers for a three-piece suite, consider covering one of the chairs in a contrasting colour. This shows up the pattern well on the settee and other chair and often creates a more satisfactory balance.

(9) If possible, try to create an integrated colour scheme for the whole house. This is not always easy to do all at once, but can be achieved gradually. Remember that each room probably opens onto another, and by carrying the colours through and linking them skilfully together a much more restful overall scheme is achieved. Colours can be linked by the choice of a basic carpet colour. If a patterned wallpaper is used in a hall, have plain walls in the rooms that open from it, or vice versa. Pick out a colour from the wallpaper in one room to create a pleasing scheme for the next, using variations in texture and amounts of colour. In this way the eye will not be confused with too many colours, and the effect will be restful and harmonious.

(10) Be aware of current trends in furnishing fashion — but only follow them if they happen to suit a particular need.

(11) Keep a scrapbook and collect cuttings of ideas and colour schemes that have special appeal and furnishing flair.

(12) Pale colours recede, deep colours appear to be closer, hence the ability to make a room look larger or smaller, narrower or wider.

(13) Dark colours give a warmer effect than light ones.

(14) Light colours create spaciousness and make a room look larger and lighter. To create the illusion of space, avoid large-patterned fabrics for walls and furnishings and also large pieces of furniture. Try to keep pattern and furniture in scale with the size of the room.

(15) Shaped pelmets and gathered valances give a room a traditional look.

(16) Draw the eye to important features in the room by using dominant colours, pattern or texture. For example, upholster a stool with a vibrant colour to emphasise its shape, or choose an unusual-shaped lampshade to draw attention to an attractive base.

(17) Chair covers or bedcovers can provide the main contrast to the basic colour chosen, and it is important that they should tone or contrast well in colour, texture and pattern.

(18) Do not be tempted to copy a room setting precisely — it can certainly be a source of inspiration, but it is much more satisfying to create an original scheme.

(19) Visit stately homes and historic houses and see how colour was used in the past. Also take note of good designs for pelmets and valances.

(20) A change is as good as a rest. If it is not possible to make major changes to a room, consider the possibility of replacing cushions or lampshades in different colours or styles. It is surprising how these small items can change the atmosphere of a room and add a new lease of life.

(21) Furnishing a room on a budget is indeed a challenge. Always be on the look out for decorative ideas that are inexpensive and simple to adapt to your needs.

2·Fabrics–Their Choice and Care

The history and development of textiles over the years is a vast and fascinating subject, and for those interested in more detailed study several comprehensive books have been written (see the Bibliography at the end of this book). It is necessary to have a sufficient knowledge of fabrics, their origin and content, to be able to select the correct fabric for each situation with confidence. It is important to know something of their different properties and their various finishes, and to be able to assess their suitability for use in soft furnishings.

Fabrics fall into two categories — natural and man-made. Natural fibres are based on raw materials from animal and vegetable sources; man-made fibres are those manufactured by chemically treating raw materials such as minerals and vegetables.

NATURAL FIBRES

Silk
Silk is the fine thread which is reeled from the cocoon of the silkworm larva, then wound on bobbins to be woven into fabric. It is manufactured mainly in the East, although France has long been renowned as the centre of silk manufacture in Europe. Silk is expensive to produce as the insects which spin the fibres are costly to rear. It has great strength but is weakened by strong sunlight. Its use has now been largely replaced by that of man-made fibres, such as rayon, as these, using vegetable cellulose, are much quicker and cheaper to produce. Silk is, therefore, a luxury fabric and is little used in soft furnishings, except for lampshades, cushions and other small accessories. It dyes extremely well and many subtle colours can be obtained. It is crease-resistant, washes well, and has a natural lustre which many other fabrics lack.

Wool
Woollen thread is produced from the twisted strands of hair shorn from the bodies of sheep, the alpaca, and some species of goat. The fibres of sheep's wool vary in length and thickness according to the breed. The coarser fibres are used for carpets and rugs; the finer fibres are made into furnishing fabrics, and are often blended with other fibres to give a crease-resistant quality. Wool is soft, warm and resilient. It is virtually uncrushable and so is a good choice for upholstery fabrics and carpets. Wool dyes well and can be rendered shrink-resistant, water-repellent, stain-repellent and mothproof. It is sometimes machine-washable.

Cotton
The cotton plant is a flowering shrub whose yellow blooms become covered with tufts of cotton wool. This is picked, carded and spun to produce cotton thread and fabric. Cotton is economic to produce, and all the fibres can be used, so there is little wastage. Strong

and hard-wearing, it washes well, and can be easily printed and dyed. Cotton fabric can be treated with several finishes and can be rendered shrink-resistant, crease-resistant, stain-repellent, drip-dry, minimum-iron, flame-proof and water-repellent. It can also be glazed, which renders the fabric dirt-resistant, and can be treated with special insulating properties which make it suitable for lining curtains. It is a versatile fabric and is often blended with other fibres. It is a very suitable choice for many items of soft furnishings.

Linen

Linen is a textile fabric woven from the fibres produced by the flax plant, which is cultivated in Northern Ireland, the Netherlands, Belgium, Russia and New Zealand. It was probably the first textile to be made by mankind, and was extensively used in ancient Egypt. It is particularly durable and hard-wearing and does not shrink but, in its natural form, creases easily. It is often blended with other fibres to give furnishing fabrics added strength. Linen has a smooth texture and does not hold the dirt. It washes easily and is stronger wet than dry, but the fibres are weakened if exposed to strong sunlight. Linen can be rendered crease-resistant, and it is particularly suitable for making loose covers because of its strength and wearing properties. It is extensively used for making tablecloths and table napkins and, in the form of buckram, for making firm lampshades.

MAN-MADE FIBRES

Great developments have recently taken place in the manufacture of man-made fibres, and progress is constantly being made in this field. New processes and techniques are being introduced to improve the properties of the fabrics, and it is often very difficult to distinguish them from the natural fibres which they imitate.

Man-made fibres are produced by chemically treating basic raw materials such as wood pulp, petroleum extracts, by-products of coal, casein, cotton linters and groundnuts. Most of the fabrics produced are not absorbent, and tend to look dirty rather more quickly than fabrics made from natural fibres. This is because the dirt stays on the surface and is not absorbed by the fabric. This makes it easy to clean. Most synthetic fibres can be blended with natural fibres or other man-made fibres to produce fabrics with varying uses and finishes, strengths and resilience.

Viscose rayon

This was the first synthetic fibre to be produced in Britain at the end of the last century. Its basic raw material is wood pulp. It is very versatile and has the appearance of silk, and was originally known as 'artificial silk'. It is easy to wash and can be rendered crease-resistant, flame-resistant and water-repellent.

Acetate rayon

This is also manufactured from wood pulp, but it is not so versatile and hard-wearing as viscose rayon. More care is needed during washing, and it will melt if subjected to high temperatures. Rayon acetate is weaker when wet and when exposed to strong sunlight. It absorbs moisture readily and so is likely to shrink.

Nylon

Hard-wearing and mothproof, nylon is made from minerals, the basic raw materials coming from coal, nitrogen and hydrogen. As it is not very durable when exposed to strong sunlight it is not suitable for curtains, but is often blended with other fibres to make suitable soft-furnishing fabrics.

Polyesters

These are produced from petroleum extracts. They are particularly suitable for curtains as the fabrics are shrinkproof, mothproof and will withstand strong sunlight. Washable wadding is also made from them and is used extensively for making continental quilts as well as pillows and cushions.

Acrylics

These are fabrics made from coal and oil and will withstand strong sunlight. They wash well and do not shrink or stretch and are therefore particularly good for making curtains. The fibres can be spun in many ways to simulate different fabrics made from natural fibres.

Glass fibre

This fabric is made from glass filaments and needs careful handling. It is used mostly for curtains and is very strong, but can be weakened if subjected to abrasion. It resists dirt well.

CHOICE OF FABRICS

When choosing and buying furnishing fabrics there are many points to remember.

(1) Buy the best-quality fabric you can afford. This may not necessarily be the most expensive, but should be the one that offers the best value for money.

(2) Buy furnishing fabrics for soft furnishing. This is what they are made for. Dress materials can sometimes be used if a special effect is needed, but they are not so durable, and as they are made in narrower widths extra care must be taken to check the requirements needed.

(3) Look at the manufacturer's label to see what claims are made. Is it shrink-resistant, fade-resistant, drip-dry, crease-resistant? If at all possible, visit the manufacturer's showrooms and see the fabrics displayed to advantage. The staff are trained to help and advise on the selection available, and this can be of great assistance when making important decisions on choice of fabrics.

(4) Make sure the fabric suits the purpose for which it is intended and that it is practical to maintain.

(5) When making loose covers choose fabric that will resist dirt well and that will not crease. It is important to choose a closely-woven fabric that is hard-wearing and washable.

(6) Curtain fabric should drape well and be fade-resistant. Always ask to see the material draped before buying it, both to check its draping qualities and the effect that light has on the fabric from the back and the front.

(7) There are many patterned fabrics of good design. Choose a well-known manufacturer and select fabrics that are printed correctly. If the pattern is not woven into the fabric, check that the design is printed correctly on the grain of the fabric. This is essential when fabric is to be used for curtains, as it is important that the bottom hem is turned up to the grain so that the curtain hangs well.

(8) Consider the pattern repeat and whether there will be much wastage. A large pattern repeat can be expensive as extra material must be allowed for matching the pattern. It is therefore more economical to choose a small pattern repeat or all-over design.

(9) Check fabrics carefully for flaws. These are usually marked on the selvedge with a coloured thread and should be allowed for by the salesman. It is important to check for flaws before cutting into the fabric as some shops will not make allowances if the material has been cut.

(10) Always look at fabrics in daylight as well as in artificial light. If possible, take a large sample home and test it in the setting for which it is intended.

(11) Consider some of the more unusual fabrics — felt, denim and mattress ticking. These are often a good choice when economy is important, or when furnishing children's bedrooms and playrooms.

(12) Make sure enough fabric is purchased for the work to be completed. It is not always possible to obtain exact colour matches at a later date.

(13) Coordinated wallpapers and fabrics can be most effective if used with care. Spend a little time experimenting with these before taking a final decision. If possible visit textile showrooms to see what can be achieved by skilful mixing and matching by colour experts.

(14) Check the 'finish' of the fabric, making sure that it has enough 'body' and that it is not just a dressing that will come out the first time the fabric is washed or dry-cleaned.

3-Tools and Equipment

Most of the tools and equipment necessary for making soft furnishings will already be in the workbox of anyone interested in needlework. However, there are some tools which are of vital importance which should not be replaced by simpler dressmaking equipment — for example, it is essential to have a meter stick in order to measure curtains and roller blinds successfully; tape measures tend to stretch with wear and it is not easy to get an accurate measurement except with a rigid rule.

Always ensure that the tools and equipment are in good working order, keeping them together tidily so that they are instantly available when needed. Remember to replenish the workbox regularly with new pins and needles — before any rust or corrosion pin-marks expensive fabric.

When buying new tools, always buy the best quality possible and use them only for the purpose for which they were intended. Never, for example, use cutting-out shears for cutting paper — keep them only for needlework. If scissors need sharpening, have them professionally ground or return them to the manufacturer. It is a specialised job that needs doing skilfully.

Pins

Use steel dressmaking pins. Steel pins do not rust and will not pin-mark fabrics. Glass-headed pins can be used, but as these are very sharp, extra care is needed when using them. Never use rusty pins. Invest in a new packet from time to time and keep them carefully in the box provided for the purpose. Do not leave pins in fabric longer than necessary, as they will mark the material if left for long periods. If a finger is pricked and blood accidentally gets on to the fabric, the best way to remove it is to chew a piece of tacking thread and rub it onto the bloodstain. This should remove the stain without leaving a water mark.

Needles

Make sure the needle is sharp and free from rust. A selection of needles of various types for different fabrics is a good investment. Use Sharps and Betweens 7-9 for general use.

Threads

Always match the thread to the fabric where possible. Use a synthetic thread with a synthetic fabric. For general use and for medium-weight fabric of linen, cotton, etc., choose Sylko 40 or 50. Use silk or no. 60 cotton on finer fabrics and tacking cotton for basting.

Scissors

A sharp pair of scissors 20-23 cm (8-9 in) long is required for cutting out, and a smaller pair 12-13cm (5-5½ in) long for cutting thread, etc. Choose the best quality possible and keep them well sharpened.

Meter stick

A wooden meter stick is an invaluable aid for measuring curtains accurately. An inexpensive one can be obtained from most wallpaper shops.

Tape measure

Choose a linen tape with a stiffened end. This will be found to be the most reliable as it will not stretch so quickly.

Tailor's chalk

This is most useful when cutting out cushions, curtains, loose covers etc. It is obtainable in off-white (which is easy to remove) and other colours.

'Quick Unpick'

This is a small tool used for unpicking stitches quickly and is a useful addition to the work-box.

Ironing board and iron

These will be in constant use. A wide board will be the most useful and a steam or heavy iron is the most suitable for soft furnishings. Man-made fibres tend to leave marks on the base of the iron, so make sure the base is cleaned regularly.

Zipper foot

This is a most useful attachment to any sewing machine and is invaluable when working with piping cord. It enables the stitching to be placed very close to the piping and ensures a neat finish. It is also used when inserting zip fasteners.

Sewing machine

It is essential to have a sewing machine for making soft furnishings as many long seams have to be worked. A hand-operated machine can be used, but an electrically operated machine will be found to be the ideal choice as both hands can then be used to control the work.

When buying a machine choose a medium/heavy-weight electric domestic machine. Light-weight portable machines are not as satisfactory for this heavier type of work, which may involve stitching through several thicknesses of fabric.

A sewing machine should last a lifetime, and much time and thought should be given to its selection. Remember that it would be pointless to choose a machine that is fully automatic, and capable of producing several embroidery stitches, if all that is required is a machine with a swing needle.

Once a decision has been made, ensure you know how the machine operates. Practise using all the attachments and learn to be in complete control of it. If possible, have some expert tuition on its correct use, and how to make the most of it. Learn to thread up the machine quickly and accurately and to change the needle to suit the fabric and thread being used. Most machines have very comprehensive instruction books, and it pays to study them carefully.

Look after the machine, and clean and oil it regularly. Keep the machine covered when not in use, and do not keep it in a cold damp room where it might rust.

4 · Basic Stitches and Techniques

It is important to have a thorough knowledge of the basic stitches and processes frequently used for soft furnishings, and it is worthwhile practising these techniques until they become automatic and can be carried out quickly and efficiently.

STITCHES

Tacking

Tacking, or basting, is temporary stitching used to hold two or more thicknesses of fabric together. Stitch from right to left. There are two types of basting: (i) long equal stitches of about 1.3 cm (½ in.) with equal space between (fig. 2); and (ii) two stitches 1.3 cm (½ in.) and one stitch 2.5 cm (1 in.) long (fig. 3). The latter is particularly useful when tacking curtains. Start and finish both types of basting with a small backstitch.

Fig. 3 **Tacking using one long and two short stitches**

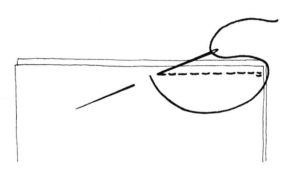

Fig. 4 **Backstitching**

Backstitch

This makes a strong seam. Stitch from right to left taking the needle back the length of the stitch behind and bringing it through the length of the stitch in front. Keep the stitching even and approximately 0.6 cm (¼ in.) in length (fig. 4). This is a useful stitch where the machine cannot work easily.

Running stitch

This is worked on the right or wrong side of

Fig. 2 **Tacking using long equal stitches**

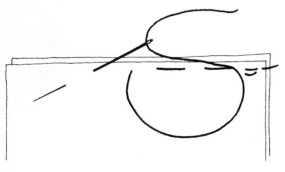

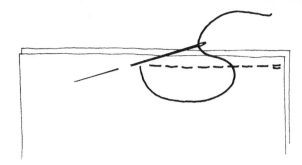

Fig. 5 **Running stitch**

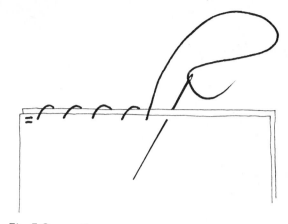

Fig. 7 **Overcasting**

the fabric from right to left. Keep the stitches even with equal spaces inbetween (fig. 5).

Blanket stitch

This is worked on the right side of the fabric from left to right. It is often used to neaten a raw edge and can be used when sewing hard lampshade fabric to the lampshade rings or frame. It can also be used as a decorative stitch. Insert the needle at right angles through the fabric and bring it out to the edge of the fabric. Make a loop by keeping the thread under the needle (fig. 6).

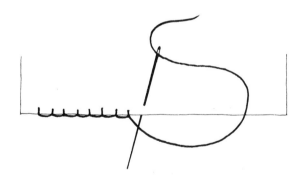

Fig. 6 **Blanket stitch**

Overcasting

This is used to neaten a raw edge to prevent fraying. Work from left to right bringing the needle through at an acute angle and taking the thread over the raw edge (fig. 7).

Slip-tacking or outside tacking

This is used for matching patterns accurately. It is particularly useful when matching patterns on curtains and can also be used when making loose covers. Fold back the edge of one piece onto the wrong side of the fabric and place onto the right side of the other piece of fabric, pinning and carefully matching the pattern. Slip-tack, taking a stitch on the fold of the one side and slipping the needle down through the fold on the other (figs. 8 and 9).

Fig. 8 **Positioning fabric for slip-tacking**

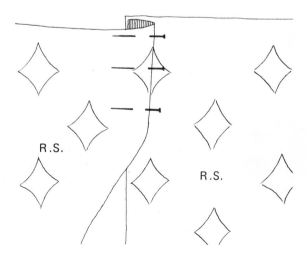

R.S.

R.S.

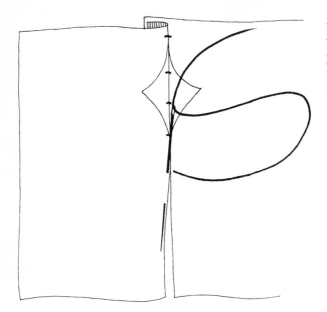

Fig. 9 **Slip-tacking**

thread from one fold and slide the needle through the fold for 0.6 cm (¼ in.), and then put the needle into the other fold and carefully draw up the thread. Do not pull tightly (fig. 11).

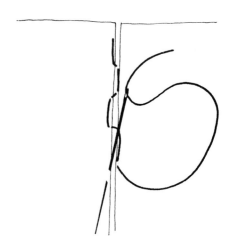

Fig. 11 **Slipstitching**

Oversewing

This is worked from right to left inserting the needle at right angles to the fabrics being joined. It can be worked using single or double thread (fig. 10).

Stab stitch

This is used to join two layers of fabric when they are too thick for a normal seam. Insert the needle at right angles, making stitches approximately 0.6 cm (¼ in.) long with an equal space between (fig. 12).

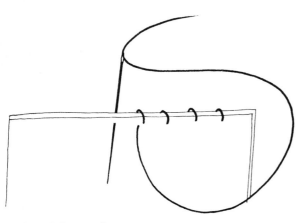

Fig. 10 Oversewing

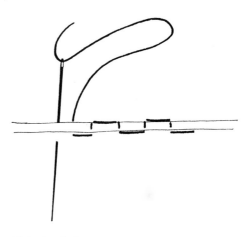

Slipstitching

This is used to join folded edges together invisibly, as on a mitred corner. Pick up a

Fig. 12 **Stab stitch**

24

Hemming

This is worked on the wrong side of the fabric and from right to left. Insert the needle just under the fold, taking a thread of fabric, and then insert the needle into the hem. Do not pull the thread tightly (figs. 13 and 14).

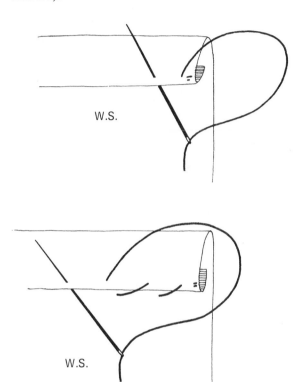

W.S.

W.S.

Figs. 13 and 14 **Hemming**

Fig. 15 **Herringbone stitch**

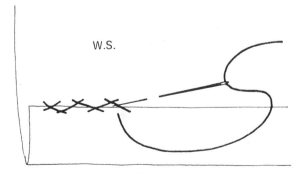

W.S.

Herringbone

This is used for making hems on heavier fabrics where extra strength is necessary, and for securing interlining to the curtain fabric when making interlined curtains. The stitch is worked from left to right usually over a raw edge. Keep the needle pointing to the left and the thread on the right-hand side of the stitching. Pick up a thread of curtain fabric and a thread of interlining alternately, keeping the stitches as near as possible to the fold (fig. 15).

Serging

This is used when turning down a single-fold hem round the edges of a curtain, before the lining is applied. Sew from left to right, picking up a thread from the fabric and then inserting the needle into the folded edge. The two stitches should be made in one movement and should be approximately 1.3 cm (½ in.) in length. The stitches should not show on the outer surface of the fabric (figs. 16 and 17).

Figs. 16 and 17 **Serging**

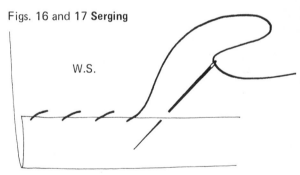

W.S.

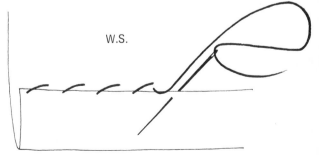

W.S.

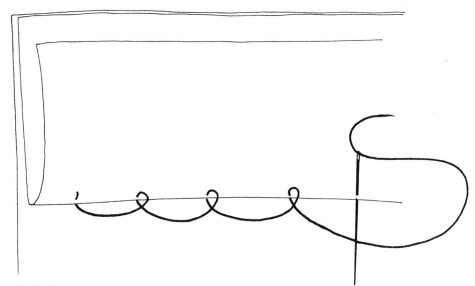

Fig. 18 **Lock stitch**

Locking

This is a long loose stitch approximately 10-15 cm (4-6 in.) in length used to 'lock' or secure the lining to a curtain. Work from left to right, using a long thread (fig. 18).

SEAMS

Plain seam

This is the most usual seam used in soft furnishings and can be worked by machine or by using a backstitch. Place the fabric with the raw edges together, right sides facing and stitch 1.3 cm (½ in.) from the edge. The seam

Fig. 19 **Plain seam**

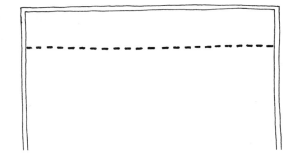

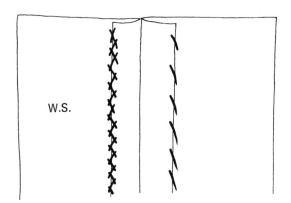

Fig. 20 **Neatening a seam with an overcasting or zigzag stitch**

is then pressed open and the edges neatened by overcasting by hand or using a zigzag stitch on the machine (figs. 19 and 20).

French seam

This seam is often used when joining widths of light-weight fabric together. It is suitable only for fabrics that are not thick and bulky. Place the two pieces of fabric together, wrong sides facing. Tack and stitch approximately 0.6-1.3 cm (¼-½ in.) from the edge, depending on whether the fabric frays easily. Trim the seam and turn to the wrong side. With right sides together tack and machine to enclose the raw edges (figs. 21 and 22).

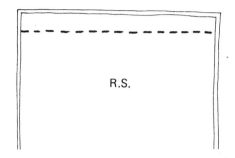

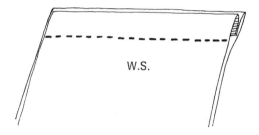

Figs. 21 and 22 **Making a french seam**

Figs. 23 and 24 **Making a run and fell seam**

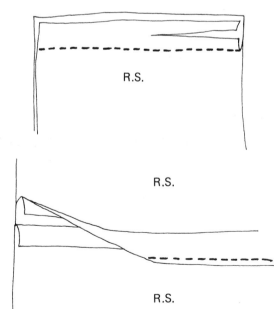

Run and fell seam

This is a useful seam when joining widths of fabric for unlined curtains. It is a strong seam and looks the same on both sides of the fabric. Place the fabric with wrong sides together and raw edges even. Tack and machine 1.3 cm (½ in.) from the edge. Press seam open. Trim one side of seam to 0.6 cm (¼ in.) and turn in raw edge of the other side 3 mm (1/8 in.). Fold this over the trimmed edge and machine close to the fold, or slip-stitch by hand (figs. 23 and 24).

PIPING AND CROSSWAY STRIP

Piping

Piping cord, covered with strips of fabric cut on the cross, is used extensively in soft furnishings. As well as being a neat, practical finish for seams, it can be used as a decorative edge. It gives added strength to seams that have constant wear, and is used to define the lines of a chair or bed when making loose covers and bedspreads.

Piping cord is usually made from cotton, and is available in various thicknesses. The thickness of the cord used must depend on the article being made and the texture of the fabric.

No. 1 (fine) This is used when making traditional down quilts or cushion covers in very fine light-weight fabrics. Use strips of crossway 3.8 cm (1½ in.) wide to cover this cord.

Nos 2, 3, 4 (medium) These are the ones used for making loose covers, cushion covers, bedspreads, etc. Use strips of crossway 3.8 cm (1½ in.) wide to cover these cords.

Nos 5, 6 (coarse) These are heavier cords and are used where thick decorative edging is required, e.g. a gathered ruche. A wider strip of fabric is required when working with these thicker cords.

Piping cord should be carefully shrunk before use — otherwise when washed it will shrink and the strips of fabric covering it will pucker. Most piping cord is sold as 'shrink-resistant', but if no guarantee of this is given, shrink it by boiling it for five minutes in a saucepan of water, and dry thoroughly before use.

Piped edge
Piping cord can be sewn along the edges of a loose cover or cushion to strengthen seams and define the shape of the article. Instructions for this technique are given on page 31.

Crossway strips
The crossway strips for covering the piping cord can be made in matching or contrasting colours, but the texture and weight of the fabric should be similar to the article being made. Loosely-woven fabric is not suitable as it wears too quickly.

To make successful piping, the crossway strips must always be cut on the true cross grain of the fabric. This is most important as any strips which are not cut to the true grain will not set properly and will not mould to the shape of the corner or curve. Fabric cut on the cross has great stretching qualities, but it will not spring back to its original size once stretched, so care must be taken with its application.

Cutting fabric on the cross
(a) Fold the material diagonally so that the selvedge thread lies across the crossways thread, i.e. the warp across the weft (fig. 25). Press.

(b) Cut along the fold. The material is then on the true bias or cross grain.

(c) In order to make all the strips the same size, make a ruler in stiff card 3.8 cm (1½ in.) wide to use as a guide. This is the most usual size of crossway strip for soft furnishings. A narrower strip 2.5 cm (1 in.) wide can be used when making a decorative trimming for a lampshade.

(d) Place the edge of the ruler to the cut edge of the fabric and mark with a sharp piece of tailor's chalk, making parallel

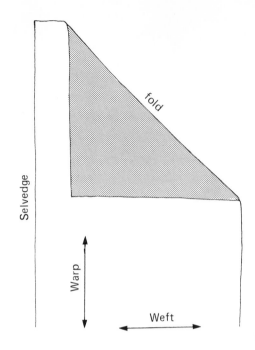

Fig. 25 **Folding fabric to make crossway strip**

Fig. 26 **Marking out the fabric using a rigid rule**

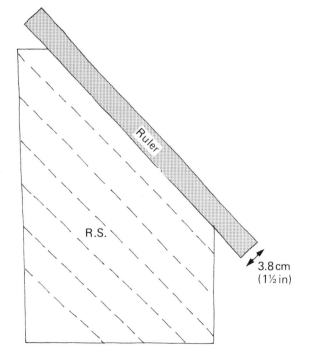

lines the same width. Cut along the lines. Continue in this way until sufficient strips have been made (fig. 26).

Joining crossway strips

All joins made on crossway strips must be made on the straight grain of the fabric. Place two strips together with right sides facing, and pin and stitch the seam with a small machine or backstitch, making sure that the strips form a V as shown in fig. 27. Press the seam open and trim away protruding ends (fig. 28).

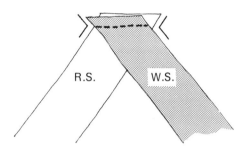

Fig. 27 **Joining crossway strips on the straight grain**

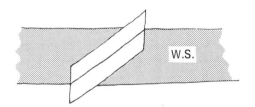

Fig. 28 **The join, pressed open**

Quick method of cutting on the cross

When a large quantity of crossway strips is required, it is useful to be able to make it without having to join each individual strip separately. Many hours of work cutting and joining the strips can be saved if the following method is used.

(a) Take a strip of fabric 23 cm (9 in.) wide. The length of the strip should be at least twice the width, i.e. 46 cm (18 in.).

(b) Fold over the top right-hand corner to obtain the direct cross (fig. 29).

Fig. 29 **Folding fabric to obtain the direct cross**

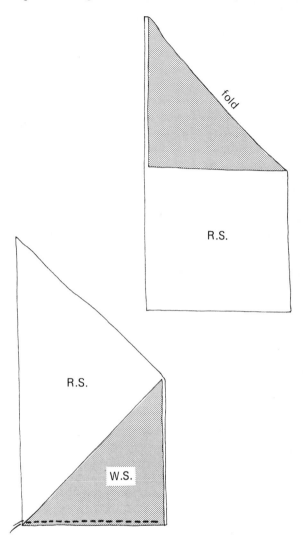

Fig. 30 **Cut off corner joined to lower edge**

(c) Cut off this corner and join to lower edge with 0.6 cm (¼ in.) seam (fig. 30). Machine this seam and press open (fig. 31). By adding this piece to the bottom no material is wasted.

(d) With a ruler 3.8 cm (1½ in.) wide, mark lines on the right side of the fabric with a sharp piece of tailor's chalk, parallel to the top edge. Mark also

29

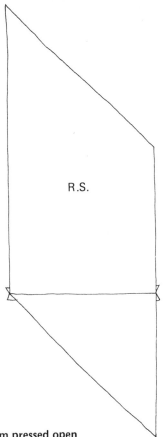

R.S.

Fig. 31 **Seam pressed open**

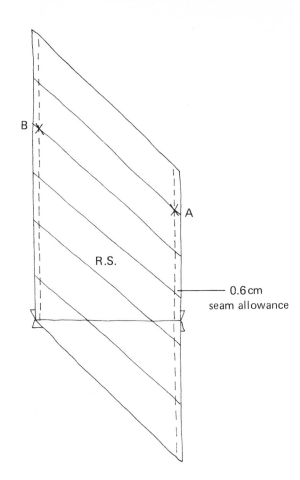

B ✕

✕ A

R.S.

— 0.6 cm
seam allowance

0.6 cm (¼ in.) seam allowance down each side, and mark the first and second lines A and B as in fig. 32.

(e) Take a pin through the wrong side of the fabric at point A and take up to point B, pinning very accurately with right sides together. Continue pinning along the seam. Tack and machine seam, checking first that the lines match exactly. This makes a tube. Press seam open, using a sleeve board (fig. 33).

(f) Turn to right side and start cutting round the tube at the projecting strip at the top edge (fig. 34).

A length of 23 cm (¼ yd.) of fabric 91 cm (1 yd.) wide makes approximately 5 m (5½ yd.) of crossway strip 3.8 cm (1½ in.) wide.

Fig. 32 **Lines marked parallel to top edge**

If plenty of fabric is available and no economy is necessary, the top right-hand corner and the bottom left-hand corner can

Fig. 33 **Tube showing seams pressed open**

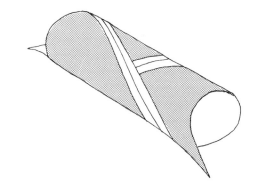

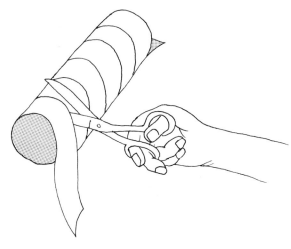

Fig. 34 **Cutting crossway strip, starting at projecting strip at the top of the tube**

Fig. 35 **Alternative method of cutting fabric**

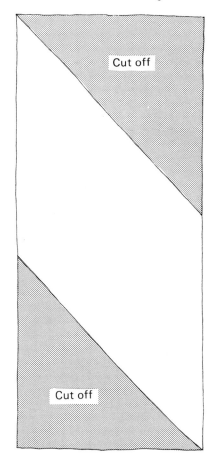

Cut off

Cut off

be cut off and discarded. This produces the same-shaped piece of fabric and has the advantage of having fewer joins in the strips. A longer and wider strip of fabric can be used (fig. 35).

Square pieces of fabric can also be utilised in a similar way by cutting and joining as in figs 36 and 37, placing AB to CD with right sides together.

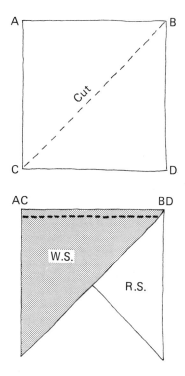

A   B

Cut

C   D

AC   BD

W.S.

R.S.

Fig.s 36 and 37 **Using a square piece of fabric**

Application of piping
Piping must be applied correctly to be successful.

(a) Cut the beginning of the crossway strip diagonally on the straight grain of the fabric.
(b) Fold the crossway strip lengthways with wrong sides together and insert the piping cord, leaving the end of the cord extending beyond the crossway strip.
(c) Start to apply the piping along a straight side — never on a corner.

31

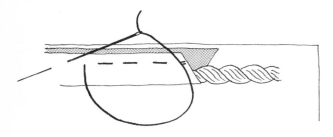

Fig. 38 Applying crossway strip and piping cord

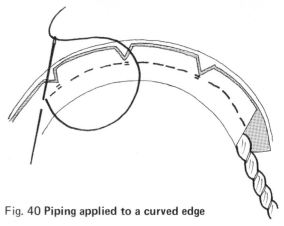

Fig. 40 **Piping applied to a curved edge**

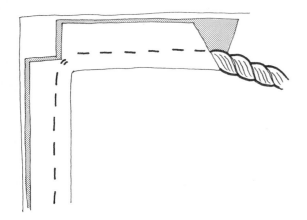

Fig. 39 **Making a slash to turn a corner**

(d) Tack with matching thread, starting with a backstitch, keeping tacking stitches close to the cord (fig. 38). These stitches remain in position and are left in the completed work.

(e) When a corner is reached only one slash is required in the crossway to turn the corner neatly. Make a clip 1.3 cm (½ in.) from the corner and make a small backstitch to strengthen it (fig. 39).

(f) To pipe round a curved edge the clips in the crossway should be made before applying the piping. This ensures that the strip moulds and sets well to the shape required. Make a backstitch at each clip for extra strength (fig. 40).

(g) Always keep the raw edges of the crossway strip level with the raw edge of the article being worked.

Joining the crossway strip

(a) To join the two ends of the piping so that they fit neatly, open the stitching at the beginning of the piping for 5 cm (2 in.). Make sure the crossway is cut diagonally across so that the edge is on the straight grain of the fabric. Mark a diagonal line 2.5 cm (1 in.) in from the raw edge using tailor's chalk, keeping the line parallel (fig. 41).

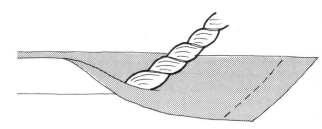

Fig. 41 **Marking a diagonal line 2.5 cm (1 in.) from raw edge**

(b) Place the other end of the crossway strip onto the chalk line, fold back onto this line and cut off (fig. 42). This gives 1.3 cm (½ in.) turnings for the seam.

(c) Join the two ends of the strip with right sides together making a 1.3 cm (½ in.) seam (fig. 43). Machine or stitch with a small backstitch. Press seam open (fig. 44).

32

Fig. 42 **Folding crossway strip at diagonal guide line**

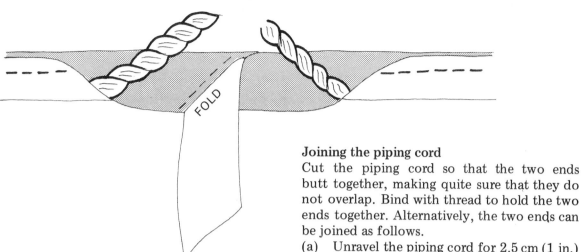

Joining the piping cord

Cut the piping cord so that the two ends butt together, making quite sure that they do not overlap. Bind with thread to hold the two ends together. Alternatively, the two ends can be joined as follows.

(a) Unravel the piping cord for 2.5 cm (1 in.) on each side.

(b) Cut away one strand from one side and two strands from the other side.

(c) Wind the remaining three strands together and stitch neatly.

Fig. 43 **Joining two crossway strips with 1.3 cm (½ in.) turnings**

Fig. 44 **Finished join in crossway strip and piping cord**

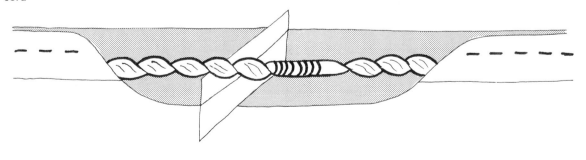

RUCHING

Gathered ruche

This produces a less tailored finish than piping and is made by covering a coarse piping cord with a strip of fabric cut on the straight grain. It can be used for decorating cushion covers, bedspreads and quilts and is most effective when used with satin or velvet.

(a) Cut strips of fabric about 7.5 cm (3 in.) wide, depending on the finished width of the trimming required. These strips should be cut on the straight of the grain from selvedge to selvedge. Join the strips by making a plain seam and pressing open. The length of the strip should be one-and-a-half to twice the length of the cord being covered.

(b) Fold the strip in half lengthwise, wrong sides together, and place the cord in the fold pinning carefully. Secure the cord to the fabric at one end to prevent it from slipping (fig. 45).

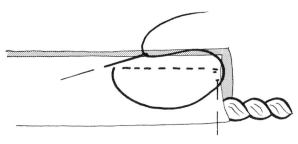

Fig. 45 **Piping cord pinned in position for a gathered ruche**

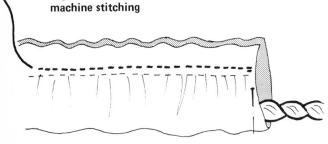

Fig. 46 **Gathered ruche, showing gathered thread and machine stitching**

(c) Make a gathering thread 1.3 cm (½ in.) from the raw edges. Draw up the thread adjusting gathers evenly (fig. 46). Machine along the line of gathering and apply to the article in the same way as a piped edge, keeping the raw edges of the ruching to the raw edges of the article.

Pleated ruche

This is another edge finish that can be used when making cushions, quilts, etc., and is a little more tailored in appearance than the gathered ruche. The size of the pleats can be adjusted to suit the fabric being used, but 1.3 cm (½ in.) pleats are usually the most suitable. The pleating can be made using knife or box pleats and many variations in size can be made.

(a) For the strip allow three times the circumference of the article to be trimmed.

(b) Cut the strip 7.5 cm (3 in.) wide on the straight grain of the fabric. Join the strips together using a plain seam and press open. Fold the strip of fabric in half lengthways and press.

(c) Make knife or box pleats in the strip of fabric, carefully marking and pinning as in figs. 47 and 48. Press and tack firmly into position.

(d) Apply to the article as for the gathered ruche, allowing extra pleats at any corners. The final join should be made when the ruche is tacked in position on the article and should be made where it is hidden in a pleat and is therefore unseen.

Flat ruche

This is not really an edge finish but a decorative border that is applied to a flat surface to cover a join. It can be used on cushions to cover the seam where two different types of fabric have been used, on quilts to define a shape, or to cover the join on the platform of a double-size fitted bedspread.

A flat ruche is made from a strip of fabric cut on the straight grain and turned in 0.6 cm

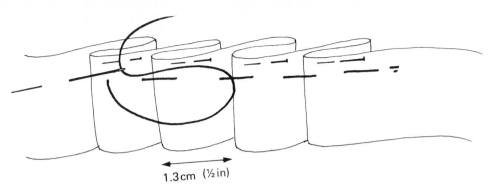

1.3cm (½in)

Fig. 47 Making a pleated ruche, showing formation of knife pleats

Fig. 48 Making a pleated ruche, showing formation of box pleats

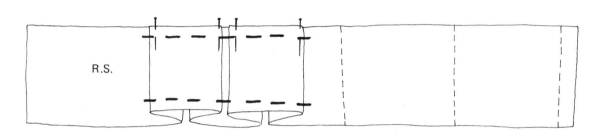

R.S.

(¼ in.) at both edges and gathered. The strip should be wide enough to cover the join and can be from 2.5 to 10 cm (1 to 4 in.) wide depending on the purpose for which it is to be used. When using a flat ruche on a bedspread the outer edge can be included in the piped seam. If a thin fabric is being used for the ruche, a strip of synthetic wadding can be inserted under the ruche to give it more body.

(a) Mark the position of the ruche with tacking lines.

(b) Cut strips of fabric on the straight grain the required width (from 2.5 to 10 cm (1 to 4 in.) plus 1.3 cm (½ in.) for turnings, and allowing one and a half times the finished length to be ruched.

Fig. 49 Applying a flat ruche, showing guide tacking lines

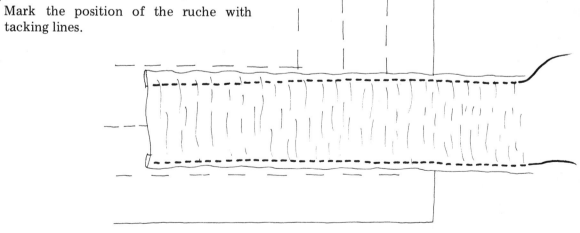

35

(c) Join the strips together with a flat seam and press open.

(d) Turn in the edges 0.6 cm (¼ in.) and make a gathering stitch 3 mm (1/8 in.) in from each edge. Draw up the gathering stitches at each side. Pin and tack to the article being ruched, adjusting the gathers carefully (fig. 49). Machine ruche along the guide tacking lines.

BOUND EDGE

This makes a very neat finish for an edge and can be both practical and decorative. It could be used to make a contrasting edge for a bedspread and, used with imagination, can have many useful applications. A bound edge is made from strips of fabric cut on the cross grain of the fabric and should be cut three times the required finished width. Usually a strip 3.8 cm (1½ in.) or 5 cm (2 in.) is wide enough.

(a) Prepare strips of fabric using the method described for cutting on page 28, or if large quantities are needed use the quick method of cutting on the cross. Remember when joining the strips together that they should be joined on the straight of the grain (figs. 27 and 28).

(b) Place the edges of the crossway strip to the right side of the edge to be bound. Tack and machine 1.3 cm (½ in.) from the edge (fig. 50).

(c) Turn the strip to the wrong side and fold

Fig. 50 **Making a bound edge, the crossway strip stitched 1.3 cm (½ in.) from raw edge**

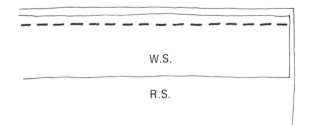

W.S.

R.S.

in 1.3 cm (½ in.). Pin and tack so that the fold comes onto the line of machine stitching. Hem by hand so that the stitches are on the machine lines (fig. 51).

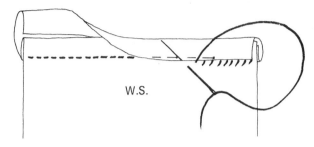

W.S.

Fig. 51 **Hemming bound edge to wrong side**

MITRED CORNERS

A mitre is used when making such items as curtains, pelmets, bedspreads, and cushions. It makes a smooth, well-defined corner that does not look bulky.

Folded mitre

Folded mitres are used on the hems of lined and interlined curtains. A perfect mitre can only be made when the two hems are the same width.

(a) Fold in the two hems the same width and press (fig. 52).

Fig. 52 **Folding and pressing hems to make a mitre**

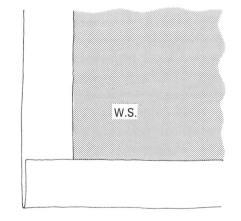

W.S.

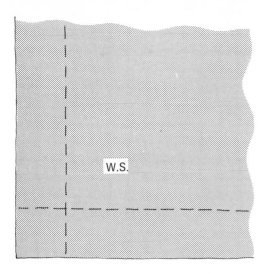

Fig. 53 **Hems opened flat to show press marks**

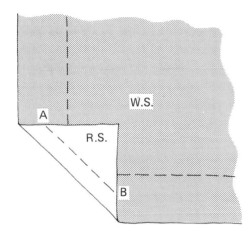

Fig. 54 **Folding the corner to make the first part of the mitre**

(b)   Open out the hems so that they are flat and the press marks are visible (fig. 53).

(c)   Fold over the right side of the corner onto the wrong side of the fabric to make the first part of the mitre (fig. 54). Press.

(d)   Fold the hem again at the side and bottom to complete the mitre (figs. 55 and 56). Slipstitch the two folds together by hand.

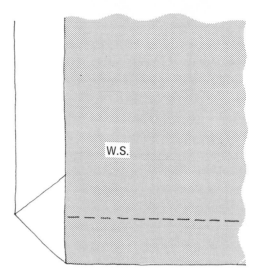

Fig. 55 **Folding in the side hem**

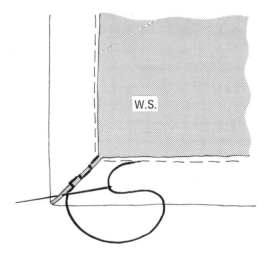

Fig. 56 **Bottom hem folded to complete the mitre and the two folds slipstitched together**

If a thick fabric is being used some of the mitre can be cut away to avoid its becoming too bulky. In this case cut from A to B as in fig. 54.

Contrast mitre

This type of mitre is used when making valances and bedspreads and also when making and applying decorative borders to curtains, loose covers and cushions.

DECORATIVE BORDERS

Making and applying a border

(a) Cut strips of fabric equal in width and overlap them at right angles (fig. 57).
(b) Make tailor tacks on a line A to B. Cut tacks.
(c) Place right sides together and pin and tack along the tailor tacking line (fig. 58).

(d) Machine along the tacking line leaving the seam open 1.3 cm (½ in.) at each end to enable the edges of the border to be turned in. Trim the seam to 1.3 cm (½ in.) and press open (fig. 59).

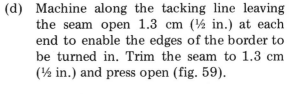

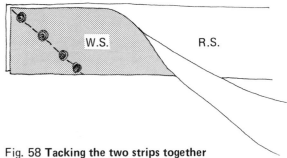

Fig. 58 **Tacking the two strips together**

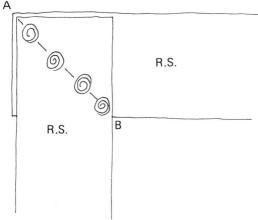

Fig. 57 **Tailor tacks made on line A — B**

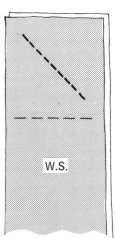

Fig. 59 **Machine line, leaving ends of seam open 1.3 cm (½ in.)**

Fig. 60 **Turning in 1.3 cm (½ in.) along raw edge, showing lines of folds**

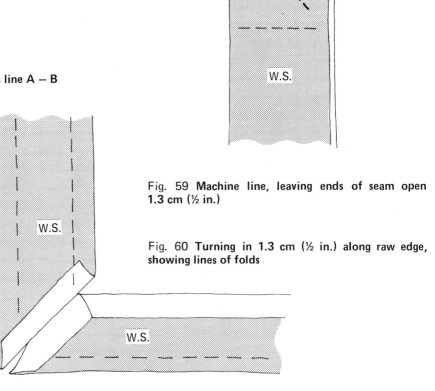

(e) Turn under and press 1.3 cm (½ in.) along the two raw edges of the border and apply to curtain, valance, etc. (fig. 60).

Applying a commercially-made border
(a) Take two lengths of decorative border of equal width and overlap them at right angles (fig. 61).
(b) Fold under both ends of the border taking great care to form the mitre at an angle of 45°(fig. 62). Press. Slip tack the two folds together.
(c) Carefully machine along the tacking line on the wrong side. Trim seams and press (figs. 63 and 64).

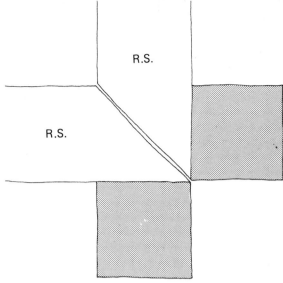

R.S.

R.S.

Fig. 62 **Borders folded to form the mitre**

Fig. 64 **Completed mitre**

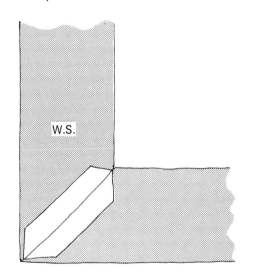

W.S.

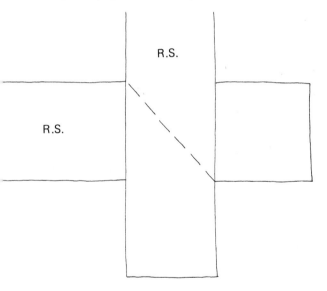

R.S.

R.S.

Fig. 61 **Overlapping two borders at right angles, showing position for mitre**

Fig. 63 **Mitre stitched at an angle of 45°**

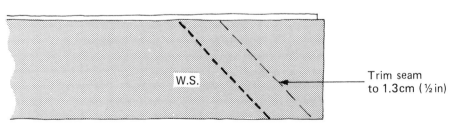

W.S.

Trim seam to 1.3cm (½in)

5-Cushions

Cushions are both decorative and functional and can give a splash of colour in a room to enhance the overall decorative scheme. A striking cushion, whether in a vibrant or contrasting colour, or made in a particularly interesting fabric or style, will attract attention.

Cushions are expensive accessories to buy, but they can be made very cheaply from remnants or odd pieces of fabrics left over from curtains, dressmaking and other home sewing. Much can be achieved with a little imagination and ingenuity, and it is surprising how one or two new cushions can change the appearance of a room, or give a lift to an old chair or settee.

If a cushion cover is being made for hard wear, care should be taken to choose a fabric that is washable. Many man-made fabrics are drip-dry and wash easily. The care of the cushion cover is governed by the fabric used; if a cover is made chiefly for decorative purposes, using for example patchwork or quilting, it would be advisable to have it dry-cleaned.

A cushion must be comfortable as well as decorative and in this respect it is only as good as its filling. A good foundation is essential for a successful cushion and care must be taken to choose the correct type of filling for both the fabric being used and the purpose for which the cushion is intended.

FILLINGS

Down
Down, the fine soft, underfeathers of birds, is an expensive filling which is very light in weight. Eider-down (from the eider duck) is the finest quality available. Down is soft, resilient, holds its shape well and is a suitable choice for cushions made from fine fabrics, such as silk or satin. About ½ kg (1 lb) of down is needed to make an average-sized cushion pad. When using down, special downproof cambric should be used for making the inner cover, so that the down does not work through the weave of the fabric.

Feathers
The larger feathers from the backs and wings of birds are much cheaper than pure down and are extensively used. On their own, they are very heavy, so they are often mixed with down to make cushions lighter in weight. The more down in the mixture, the more expensive the filling. Feather-proof ticking must be used for the inner cover to prevent the feathers working through. About 1 kg (2 lb.) of feathers is needed to make an average-sized cushion pad.

Kapok
Kapok, a silky vegetable fibre cultivated in Java and Ceylon, is very light in weight and inexpensive, but tends to go lumpy with

40

wear. The kapok should be teased apart before use to avoid this happening. As it does not absorb moisture it is very satisfactory for garden cushions. Kapok does not work through fabric, so a special inner cover is not necessary. About ½ kg (1 lb) of kapok is enough to fill a small cushion.

Man-made fibre

Man-made fibres such as Terylene, Dacron and Courtelle are inexpensive and non-absorbent. This filling is washable and will not work through the inner cover. About ½ kg (1 lb) will fill an average-sized cushion. Use a washable fabric to make the inner cover so that the cushion is completely washable.

Latex and plastic foam

Latex and plastic foam can be obtained in various shapes, sizes and thicknesses. It varies in quality and can be cut to the exact size required with a very sharp knife. It keeps its shape well, but should be covered with a calico inner cover to protect it from wear and from sunlight.

Plastic foam chips

These can be used as an inexpensive filling for cushion pads, but they do not have the same smooth appearance as other more costly fillings. They are particularly suitable for garden cushions as they do not absorb moisture.

THE CUSHION PAD

Choice of fabric

The type of fabric needed to make the inner cover, or cushion pad, should be governed by the type of filling being used.

Downproof cambric

This fabric is specially waxed on the wrong side to prevent the down from working through. A double row of machine stitching on all seams also helps to keep the down enclosed. If a piece of beeswax is available, rub this over the seam for extra protection.

Feather-proof ticking

If black and white ticking is used make sure that this will not show through the top cushion cover fabric.

Calico

Bleached or unbleached calico can be used where extra strength is necessary. As latex and plastic foam are affected by sun and light, this is a most suitable fabric to use for making the inner cover for these fillings.

Remnants

Remnants of sheeting, curtain lining, etc., can be used for making inner covers, provided the fillings are suitable.

Making the pad

To make sure that the finished cushion has a well-filled appearance, make the inner pad 1.3 cm (½ in.) larger all round than the outer cushion cover. This means that on a 38 cm (15 in.) square cushion the finished inner pad should measure 40.5 cm (16 in.). This applies only when making cushions with loose fillings such as down, feather, kapok, etc. When making an inner cover for a latex or plastic-foam shape, the inner case must be made to the exact size, as this filling is more rigid and firm.

Cut two pieces of fabric the size required, allowing 1.3 cm (½ in.) turnings for seams. Place the right sides together and machine round the four sides leaving an opening of approximately 20 cm (8 in.) on one side. Turn the cover to the right side and fill. Sew up the opening with oversewing stitches.

THE OUTER COVER

The outer cover can be made from many different fabrics ranging from dress fabrics to heavy furnishing fabrics. Subtle colours in silks and man-made fibres can often be obtained in the dress fabric departments and make most attractive decorative cushion covers.

Delicate fabrics lend themselves to decorative edges such as ruching and pleating, but heavier furnishing fabrics look best when tailored with a piped or boxed edge.

Cushions can be made in all shapes and sizes. Square cushions vary in size from 38 cm (15 in.) upwards, depending on the purpose for which they are required. Round cushions can be made to any size, with or without a boxed edge, and can be made to fit a chair seat with or without ties. Variations can be made by cutting out shapes in triangles, diamonds, hearts, etc. Always make a paper pattern first before cutting into the fabric, remembering that the filling will take up some of the fabric. The pattern will need to be cut slightly larger to allow for this.

OPENINGS

All cushion covers need an opening, but this does not necessarily need to be permanent. A neater finish is obtained by slipstitching the opening together when the cushion pad has been inserted, and this method can be used on all cushions that are purely decorative. If, however, the cover needs to be removed regularly for laundering or dry cleaning, it obviously needs to have a more permanent type of opening.

Always leave the opening large enough to enable the cushion pad to be slipped inside easily. It is usually made to come within 2.5 cm (1 in.) of the two corners on one side. The opening should show as little as possible, and should therefore be placed at the most inconspicuous position on the cushion cover. As a rule these will be as follows.

(i)   Square or rectangular scatter cushions — opening to be along the bottom of the pattern (fig. 65 i).
(ii) Square seat cushions — opening to be along the back edge of the cushion, i.e. at the top of the pattern (fig 65 ii).
(iii) Round seat cushion — opening to be

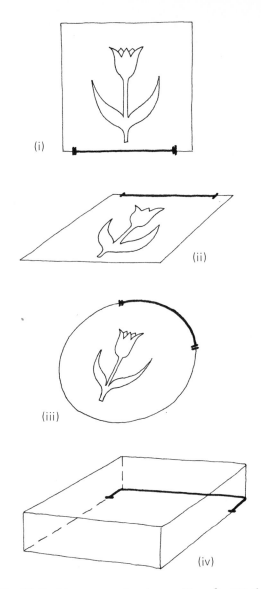

Fig. 65 **Cushion covers showing positions for openings (i) Scatter cushion (ii) Square seat cushion (iii) Round seat cushion (iv) Boxed seat cushion**

towards the back of the cushion at the top of the pattern (fig. 65 iii).

(iv) Square and rectangular boxed seat cushions — opening to be along the bottom edge of the back of the cushion, extending round to each side 5-7.5 cm (2-3 in.) (fig. 65 iv).

When a permanent type of opening is necessary, choose from the following.

Strap and facing
Use this on a square or rectangular cushion cover where slipstitching is impractical and a permanent opening is necessary.

Continuous wrap opening
This is used for box cushions where the back is not shaped, and also for loose covers where an opening is necessary (see detailed instructions on page 49). To give extra strength, hooks and bars and snap fasteners should be used with this type of opening.

Zip fasteners
Zip fasteners make a neat finish on some cushions if applied with care. Make sure a long enough zip is used so that there is not undue strain on the zip when the cushion pad is removed. The zip should be 5 cm (2 in.) shorter than the side of the cushion where it is being inserted. Always insert the zip along the piped edge of the cushion cover in the seam of the cover and not in the middle of the welt or centre back of the cover, since this makes the opening too conspicuous.

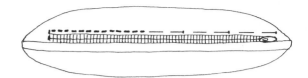

Fig. 67 **Right side of cushion cover showing insertion of zip fastener**

Zips can be inserted by machine, using the zipper foot, or stitched by hand using a small backstitch.

When applying a zip fastener to a piped opening, use the following method
(a) Open the zip and pin and tack the piped edge to one side of the zip, right sides together. Tack 3 mm (1/8 in.) from the teeth of the zip (fig. 66). Machine or backstitch by hand.
(b) Close the zip and pin and tack the other side of the zip to the 1.3 cm (½ in) turning, making sure that the fold covers the teeth of the zip. Machine or stitch by hand 3 mm (1/8 in.) from the teeth (fig. 67).

Velcro
Velcro is a 'touch and close' fastening which is made in the form of two tapes or surfaces. One surface is covered with a nylon fuzz, and the other is covered with tiny nylon hooks, which catch onto the fuzz when the two surfaces are pressed together. To open again, one simply pulls the surfaces apart. A strip of each surface is sewn onto each side of the opening on the seam allowance. Velcro is suitable for use on cushion cover and loose cover openings, but is rather more expensive than zip fasteners, hooks and bars, and snap fasteners. It can be used in many other situations, and it washes and dry cleans well.

BASIC CUSHION COVERS

These are some of the basic methods of making cushion covers, using different techniques. Once these techniques have been

Fig. 66 **Zip fastener tacked to piped edge of cushion cover**

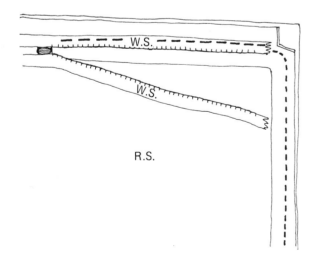

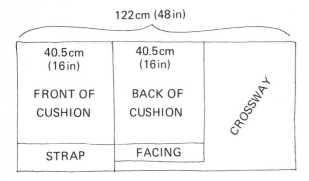

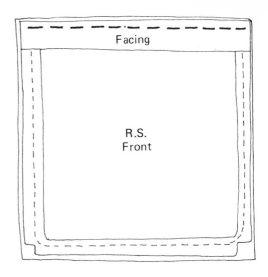

Fig. 68 **Cutting out plan for square piped cushion with strap and facing**

mastered, many adaptations can be made to suit individual requirements.

Square piped cushion cover with strap and facing

(a) Prepare a cutting out plan as in fig. 68.

(b) Cut two pieces of fabric the size of the cushion plus 1.3 cm (½ in.) turnings on all sides. If the material is patterned make sure any motif is centralised.

(c) Cut a 7.5 cm (3 in.) wide strap and a 5 cm (2 in.) wide facing as in the cutting plan (fig. 68). The remaining fabric can be used for making a crossway strip.

(d) Prepare enough crossway strip to go round the four sides of the cushion, plus a little extra. Use the quick method described on page 29.

(e) Apply the crossway strip and the piping cord to the front section of the cover on the right side, as on page 31, tacking and machining close to the cord.

(f) Place the 5 cm (2 in.) wide facing along the opening edge of the cushion cover front section, with right sides together. Tack and machine close to the piping cord using a zipper foot, and taking 1.3 cm (½ in.) turnings (fig. 69).

(g) Turn the facing to the wrong side of the cover and fold under 1.3 cm (½ in.) at the bottom edge. Tack and hem as in fig. 70.

Fig. 69 **Facing tacked to front section of cushion cover**

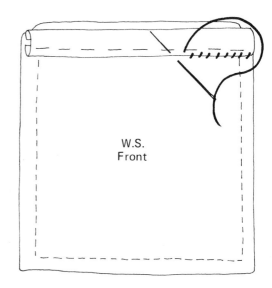

Fig. 70 **Facing hem stitched to wrong side of front section**

(h) Apply the 7.5 cm (3 in.) wide strap to the back section of the cushion cover. Tack and machine, taking 1.3 cm (½ in.) turnings. Fold over 1.3 cm (½ in.) and place on line of stitching. Tack and hem in position (fig. 71).

44

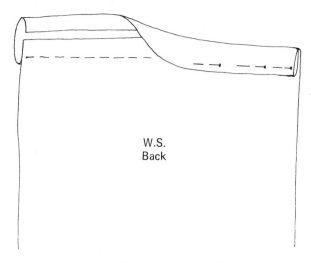

Fig. 71 **Strap tacked to back section of cover**

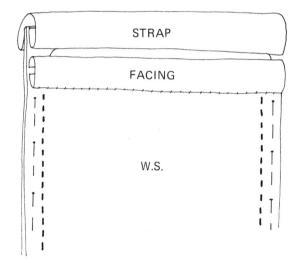

Fig. 72 **Strap extending above facing**

(i)   Place the back section of the cushion cover to the front section with right sides together, with the strap extending above the facing (fig. 72). Pin round the other three sides, tacking and machining as close as possible to the piping cord, using a zipper foot. Neaten the raw edges.

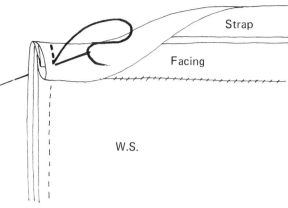

Fig. 73 **Stabstitching the strap over the facing**

(j)   Turn the strap over onto the facing at the two sides and stab stitch down the seam line for 2.5 cm (1 in.) (fig. 73).

(k)   Turn the cushion cover to the right side and mark the position for the hooks and bars 2.5 cm (1 in.) from each end and 5 cm (2 in.) apart.

(l)   Sew on hooks using buttonhole stitch, covering each ring. Finish with a backstitch.

(m)   If you do not have metal or plastic bars make them from thread. Use double matching thread. Start with a backstitch and make two 3 mm (1/8 in.) long stitches for the bar (fig. 74). Tighten stitches firmly and blanket stitch over loop as in fig. 74. Finish with a small backstitch.

Fig. 74 **Making a bar using a double thread**

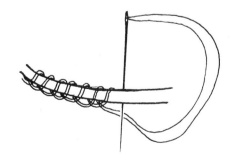

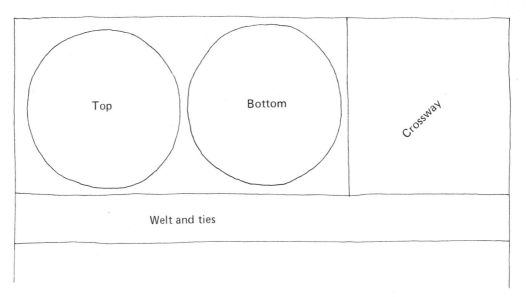

Fig. 75 **Cutting out plan for round squab seat cushion**

Round squab seat cushion with
welt and ties

(a) Make a paper pattern the size of the cushion required and prepare a cutting out plan (fig. 75).

(b) From the pattern cut two circles for the top and bottom sections of the cushion cover, allowing 1.3 cm (½ in.) turnings all round. Cut a strip of fabric on the straight grain from selvedge to selvedge for the welt. This must be cut the required depth plus 1.3 cm (½ in.) turnings on each edge, and the length must be the circumference of the circle plus 10 cm (4 in.) for seam allowance and easing.

(c) Prepare enough crossway strip 3.8 cm (1½ in.) wide for piping round the top and bottom sections of the cover (i.e. twice the circumference) plus a little extra.

(d) Apply the crossway strip and piping cord by pinning and tacking to the top and bottom sections of the cover, clipping at frequent intervals to allow the piping to mould to the shape of the cover (fig. 76). Machine.

(e) Pin and tack the welt to the top section of the cover, right sides together and find the exact position for the join in the welt (fig. 77). Machine stitch seams, using a zipper foot, keeping the stitching as close as possible to the piping cord.

Fig. 76 **Tacking the piping to the top and bottom sections of the cushion cover**

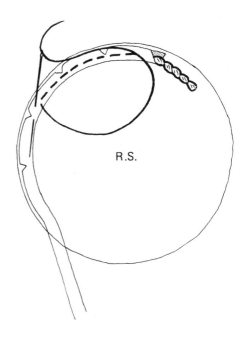

R.S.

46

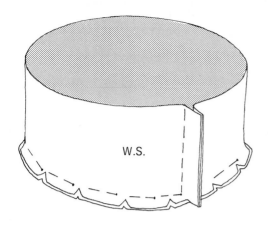

Fig. 77 **Making the join in the welt**

(f) To make ties, cut 3 cm (1¼ in.) wide strips of fabric on the straight grain long enough to make two ties — approximately 60 cm (24 in.). Fold in half lengthwise and press. Turn in all edges 0.6 cm (¼ in.) and press. Machine all round. Mark positions for the ties on the bottom section of the cover and apply as in fig. 78 to the right side.

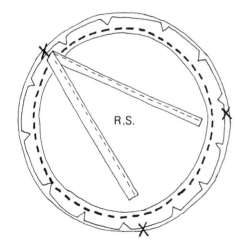

Fig. 78 **Positions for ties marked with an X**

(g) Pin and tack the welt to the bottom section of the cushion cover (fig. 77) leaving an opening at the back edge of

the cover. This should be large enough to insert the pad. Machine seam.

(h) Neaten the raw edges by overcasting, or machine using a zigzag stitch.

(i) Insert the cushion pad into the cover and slipstitch the opening together.

Box cushion with continuous wrap opening
Most armchairs have boxed seat cushions. Whatever their shape and size, they all have a welt of 5-10 cm (2-4 in.) between the top and bottom sections of the cushion cover. The pads for these covers often have a sprung interior, or are made from foam rubber, which makes them more rigid than those filled with down or feathers. When making covers for these cushions it is therefore necessary to have a larger opening to enable the pad to be easily inserted. The opening is at the back of the cushion and extends round the sides for 5-10 cm (2-4 in.). This measurement should be determined by the depth of the welt (see fig. 65 iv). When measuring for these covers remember to take the exact measurement of the pad as this is rigid, and add to this 1.3 cm (½ in.) all round for turnings.

(a) Prepare a cutting plan to estimate the amount of fabric required (fig. 79).

(b) Cut out the fabric following the plan allowing 1.3 cm (½ in.) turnings on all pieces, and centralising any pattern. If the cover is to be used for a seat cushion for a chair the pattern should match that of the inside back and the seat of the chair cover.

(c) Tack the top and bottom sections in the centre, with right sides together, to hold the two pieces firmly in position (fig. 80).

(d) Pin each welt in separately, placing right sides together. Start tacking 2.5 cm (1 in.) from the edge of the fabric and 2.5 cm (1 in.) from the edge of the welt (fig. 81). Tack and machine corner seams of welt to within 1.3 cm (½ in.) of each edge, taking 1.3 cm (½ in.)

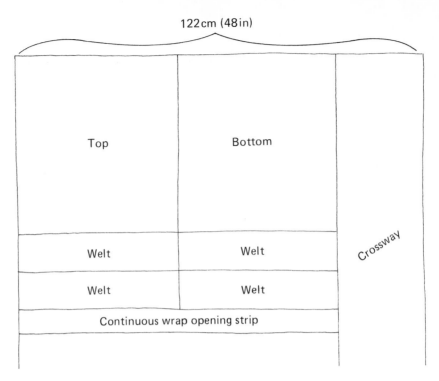

122 cm (48 in)

Top

Bottom

Welt

Welt

Crossway

Welt

Welt

Continuous wrap opening strip

Fig. 79 **Cutting out plan for a box cushion**

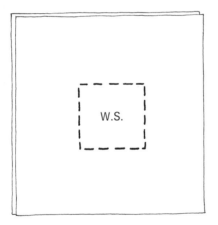

W.S.

Fig. 80 **Tacking the top and bottom sections together**

turnings (fig. 82). Press these four corner seams open.

(e) Apply crossway strip and piping cord to the top and bottom sections of the cover, inserting it between the welt and the top and bottom sections (fig. 83). Pin and tack, clipping corners. Machine round the top section using a zipper foot, stitching as close as possible to the piping cord. The bottom section of the cushion cover must be left open to allow for the continuous wrap opening

Fig. 81 **Tacking in the welt 2.5 cm (1 in.) from raw edges**

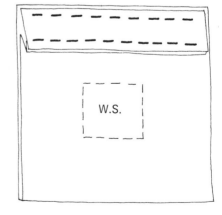

W.S.

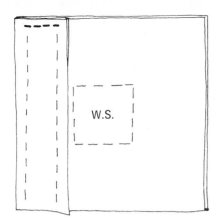

Fig. 82 **Corner seam of welt stitched to within 1.3 cm (½ in.) of each edge, allowing 1.3 cm (½ in.) turnings**

Fig. 83 **Piping applied between welt and bottom section of cover**

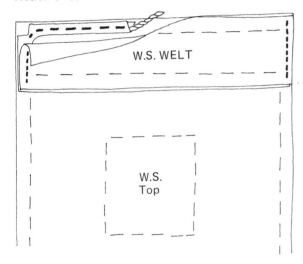

(a) Cut a length of fabric twice the length of the opening plus 2.5 cm (1 in.). The width of the strip should be 6.5-7.5 cm (2½-3 in.). Join the strip at the short sides with 1.3 cm (½ in.) turnings.

(b) Pin the right side of the strip to the right side of the cushion cover opening taking 1.3 cm (½ in.) turnings (fig. 84). Tack and machine.

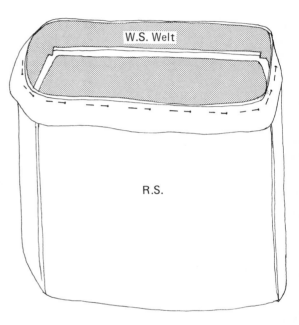

Fig. 84 **Strip pinned to the right side of the cushion cover opening**

(c) Along the unpiped edge of the opening cut away 1.3 cm (½ in.) of fabric from the strip (fig. 85). Turn down 1.3 cm (½ in.) along this cut-away side and fold over to the wrong side, then hem stitch to the welt (fig. 86).

(d) On the piped side of the opening turn over the strip 1 3 cm (½ in.) and fold over onto the line of machine stitching. Pin, tack and hem along this line of stitching (fig. 87).

(e) Stitch across firmly on fold at both ends of the opening at A (fig. 88).

along the back seam and the extension along each side of 5-10 cm (2-4 in.). The remaining seams of the bottom section can then be stitched, machining as close as possible to the piping cord.

(f) Take out all the tacking stitches and turn the cushion cover to the right side.

Making the continuous wrap opening

This is a strong, inconspicuous opening suitable for box cushion covers. It can also be used for openings on loose covers.

49

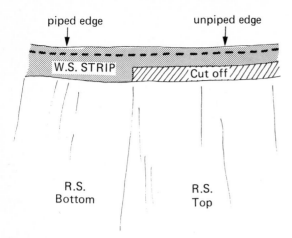

Fig. 85 **Cutting away fabric along the unpiped edge of the strip**

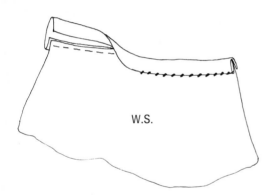

Fig. 86 **Hem stitching strip on unpiped edge**

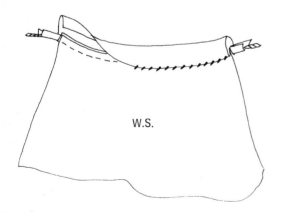

Fig. 87 **Hem stitching strip on line of stitching on piped edge**

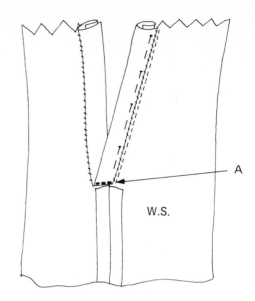

Fig. 88 **Stitching across the end of the opening on the wrong side**

(f) Mark positions for hooks and bars and snap fasteners. These should be sewn 3.8 cm (1½ in.) apart, alternately along the opening.

(g) Neaten raw edges at inside of cushion and press.

Bolster cushions

Bolster cushions have many uses and are very decorative when used in the garden or bedroom. They vary in size from 15 to 20 cm (6 to 8 in.) in diameter and from 40 to 75 cm (16 to 30 in.) long. Covers can be made in a combination of fabrics with various edge finishes to produce interesting effects, or can be made perfectly plain with a piped edge or a gathered end. Avoid using fabrics with large patterns as these may be difficult to match at the seams.

Bolster cushion with piped ends

(a) Cut two circles the size required allowing 1.3 cm (½ in.) turnings all round. These circular ends should be cut from a paper pattern. Use a large plate or a lampshade frame to make the pattern.

(b) Cut a rectangle of fabric on the straight grain, the circumference plus 2.5 cm (1 in.) for turnings, and the required length of the cushion cover.

(c) With right sides together pin, tack and machine at each end of the long sides of the rectangle, leaving an opening at the centre (fig. 89). A zip fastener can be inserted in the opening, or this can be slipstitched together when the pad has been inserted.

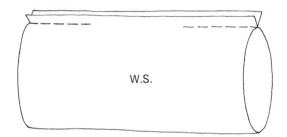

Fig. 89 **Stitching the rectangle to make a bolster cushion**

(d) Apply crossway strip and piping cord to the two circular ends clipping the crossway to enable it to mould to the shape of the curve (fig. 76).

(e) Pin and tack the circular ends to the tube with right sides together, snipping the seam allowance at intervals (fig. 90).

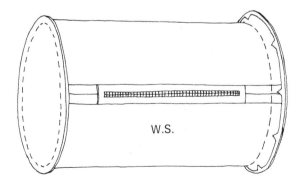

Fig. 90 **Circular ends tacked in position on bolster cushion**

Machine, using a zipper foot, stitching as close as possible to the piping cord.

(f) Turn the cushion cover to the right side through the opening. Neaten raw edges and press. Insert the pad and slipstitch the opening together.

Bolster cushion with gathered ends
A gathered end can be made for the bolster by cutting a strip of fabric on the straight grain as long as the circumference of the circle plus 2.5 cm (1 in.), and as wide as its radius. Join the short ends of the strip together and tack one long edge to the tube. Run a gathering stitch 1.3 cm (½ in.) in from the inner edge of the circle and draw it up tightly to fit the centre of the circle (fig. 91). Fasten off ends securely. To neaten the centre, sew a covered button or tassel over the raw edges at each end of the cushion cover.

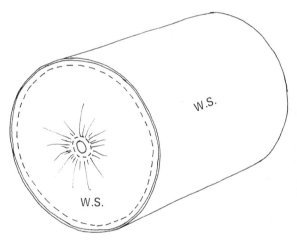

Fig. 91 **Making a gathered end for a bolster cushion**

Buttoning a cushion cover
Covered buttons can be used on many types of cushion covers and make an attractive, decorative feature. Commercially made moulds can be used or shapes can be cut in strong cardboard or thin plywood. Pad the top of the shape with wadding and cover as for a commercial mould. On a purely decorative cushion, the fabric used for covering the

51

buttons could first be decorated with beads or embroidery.

Covering a button mould

Cut a piece of fabric 1.3 cm (½ in.) larger than the button mould. Make a running stitch round the end of the fabric and draw up to fit over the mould (figs. 92 and 93).

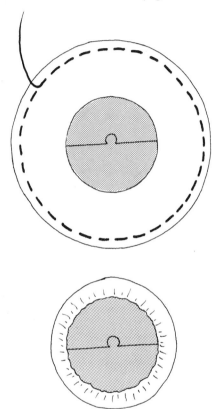

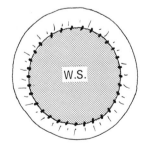

Figs. 92 and 93 **Covering a commercial button mould**

Fig. 94 **Covering the back of a hand-made button**

Fasten off securely. To cover the back of the button cut a smaller piece of fabric, turn in the edge and slipstitch to the back of the button (fig. 94).

Buttoning down a cushion

Mark the centre of the cushion cover on both sides. Using double button thread and a long darning needle secure thread to the back of one button in the position marked. Take the thread through to the other side of the cushion cover to the point marked, and into the back of the second button. Take the thread back to the first button and pull tightly so that the buttons sink into the cover. Knot and fasten off securely.

Oblong cushion using remnants

This is an effective style of cushion cover and can be made from small pieces of fabric left over from other major projects. When using striped fabric, care must be taken to make sure that the stripes match correctly.

Fig. 95 **Centre panel stitched to the two end panels, with decorative braid being stitched into position**

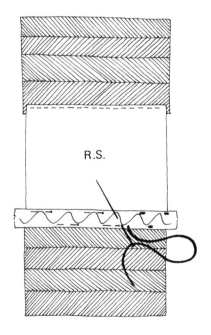

(a) Cut two pieces of fabric for the centre panels approximately 18 cm x 25.5 cm (7 in. x 10 in.), and four pieces the same size for the end panels. Make sure any stripes are positioned so that they match exactly.

(b) Pin and tack the centre panel to the two outer panels using a lapped seam to make the top section of the cushion cover (fig. 95). Machine.

(c) Sew the bottom section of the cover in exactly the same way, taking care to match up any stripes.

(d) Pin a decorative braid over the four lapped seams of the top and bottom sections and sew into position using a zigzag type stitch (fig. 95).

(e) Place the top and bottom sections together with right sides facing. Pin and tack round three sides, leaving one short side unstitched for the opening (fig.96). Machine. Neaten raw edges.

(f) Turn cushion cover to the right side and apply trimmings to each end of the cover. Turn in raw edges of trimming 1.3 cm (½ in.) and butt the ends together. Fringing can be used on the top section of the cover together with matching braid on the bottom section (fig. 97).

(g) Insert the cushion pad and slipstitch the opening together.

Fig. 96 **Three sides of the cushion cover stitched in position**

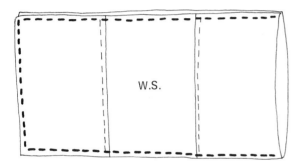

Fig. 97 **Finished cushion cover showing use of fringing and braid**

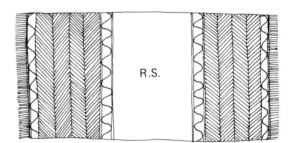

6-Curtains

WINDOW TREATMENTS

Well planned window treatments can do much to furnish a room, as together with floor and wall coverings they provide the greatest expanse of colour and texture, and often set the atmosphere of the room. Many architectural faults can be disguised, if not remedied, by the clever use of curtaining. Much can be done to create illusions of width, height and shape if careful thought is given to the planning and treatment of windows and doors.

First it is important to consider whether the window is in proportion to the size of the room — is it too high or too low? Is there sufficient light filtering into the room? If there is insufficient light, together with a low ceiling, it would obviously be unwise to cut out more light by using a pelmet or valance. The most intense light enters a room from ceiling height and so, in this case, a decorative heading or rod would be the best choice.

If a window is not of pleasing proportions, an illusion of length or width can be obtained in many ways: using floor length curtains; extending the rail several inches at each side of the window frame so that the curtains actually hang against the wall and not the window; having the rail well above the window frame, etc. If a window is considered too wide, the curtains can be hung inside the frame so that they hide part of the window.

A large picture window from ceiling to floor obviously needs floor-length curtains. Give these interest by using a decorative heading to cover the track. In this situation avoid pelmets and valances and also make sure that the curtain rail extends well beyond the window frame in order to take full advantage of the large expanse of glass and the light that it offers.

Bay windows often present difficulties when planning curtains. They need to be treated quite separately from other windows and doors in the room. If possible, use one pair of full length curtains. If, however, it is necessary to have more than two curtains, a pelmet or valance helps to give an overall effect and brings the whole unit together.

If there are several small windows along one wall, consider treating them as a whole and using one long track. Arrange the curtains so that they cover the blank walls in the daytime. At night when the curtains are drawn, this type of treatment displays a large expanse of colour or texture instead of several small areas. The use of a pelmet or valance here would also help to create an overall effect.

Curved windows and archways can be treated by using a flexible track which can be rounded to the shape of the window. These tracks are also useful when fixed round dressing tables and vanitory units.

Without doubt most curtains look more attractive if they are made to floor length, unless there is an obstacle immediately beneath such as a window seat or a radiator.

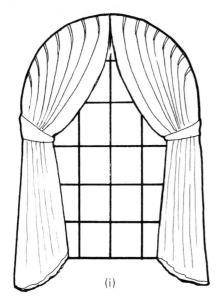

(i)

If the view from a window is unattractive, it may be preferable to use café curtains or roller blinds. Cafe curtains are generally less costly, as only half of the window is curtained and less fabric is needed. Roller blinds

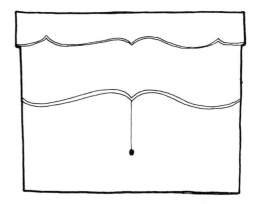

Fig. 99 **Matching design for a roller blind and pelmet**

(ii)

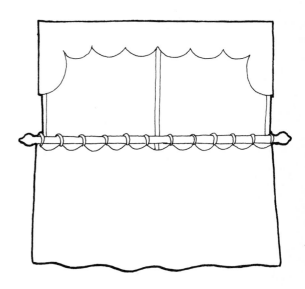

fig. 100 **Matching pelmet and café curtain**

Fig. 98 **Two treatments of a curved window: (i) use of flexible aluminium track (ii) shaped pelmet taking the shape of the window**

Floor length curtains do, of course, require a considerable amount of fabric, and therefore the choice of material and its cost must be considered carefully.

are economical if made at home, and can be the most practical way of treating kitchen and bathroom windows. Both blinds and café curtains can be used most effectively in conjunction with pelmets or valances to create an original and interesting scheme.

Curtain tracks and fittings

There are so many different decorative tracks, rods, poles and fittings available that it is often difficult to know which to choose.

It is advisable to visit a reputable soft furnishing or hardware shop to see the range of fittings displayed. Here expert help will be given and advice can be obtained on the type of fittings best suited to each particular window. Several manufacturers provide useful booklets and leaflets to help with the choice of curtain tracks and accessories, and these are well worth studying before a final choice is made. Most large soft furnishing departments have good displays of curtain hardware, and it is important to be able to compare their differences and to understand their varying functions.

To achieve a satisfactory result, there are several points which should be borne in mind before a selection is made.

(1) Decide on the type of effect required — traditional or contemporary.

(2) Choose the type of fabric and the style of curtain appropriate to the room, the aspect and the decorative scheme. This governs the choice of the quality and type of the track since some plastic tracks are not made to take the weight of heavy velvet or interlined curtains, but are perfectly satisfactory for light-weight curtains. Check, therefore, that the tracks and fittings are strong enough to carry the weight of the curtains they are to support.

(3) There is a wide variety of finishes to decorative poles and tracks and their accessories (rings, hooks, brackets, etc.). Decide whether a wooden, brass, pewter, or anodised aluminium finish is required, and whether a pole or a track best suits the window.

(4) Decide on the heading. This must depend to some extent on the choice of fabric. For example, if a striped brocade is chosen, much of the pattern will be lost at the heading if a pinch pleated style is chosen; spaced groups of pleats, however, would show the fabric off to the best advantage.

(5) If a pelmet or valance is being used the heading of the curtains will be covered and therefore only a gathered type of heading is necessary. This is very economical as less fabric is required.

Choice of fabrics

Great care should be taken to select a fabric that suits both the decorative scheme and the purpose for which the curtains are needed.

(1) Make sure the curtain fabric is fadeless, as it is very often exposed to strong sunlight. If unlined curtains are being made remember that the fabric will not have the protection of a lining, so check that the fabric is under guarantee.

(2) Curtain fabric must drape well. Always ask to see the fabric draped, to check both its draping qualities and also its colour and pattern. Patterns and colours look quite different when lying flat on a table. Also look at the fabric both in daylight and in artificial light.

(3) Only buy fabric that is recommended for curtains. For example, upholstery fabrics are often too heavy to drape well and may also crease badly because of their high linen content.

(4) Check whether the fabric needs dry cleaning or whether it is washable only, in which case is it shrink-resistant?

(5) When buying patterned fabric check that the pattern is printed correctly on the grain of the fabric if it is not woven into the fabric. This is a fault that can present serious problems when making up, as each length of curtain should be cut to the grain of the fabric to make it hang well.

(6) When choosing patterned fabric remember that more is needed in order to match the pattern correctly. Small pattern repeats are therefore more economical than large ones as much

wastage can occur. An allowance of one pattern repeat to each length or 'drop' of curtain, should be made.

(7) Check that the fabric is free from flaws. These are usually marked with a coloured cotton on the selvedge and should be allowed for by the sales assistant.

(8) Buy enough fabric to complete the curtains. It is not always possible to obtain exact colour matches if extra fabric is needed afterwards.

(9) Make a sketch of the window to be curtained showing accurate measurements and take this to the shop when buying fabric.

Linings

All curtains, with the exception of simple kitchen and bathroom curtains, are generally enhanced by a lining. As well as enabling the curtain to drape well, it helps to protect the curtain fabric against strong sunlight, dust, dirt and frost. All these damage the fibres of the fabric and therefore make it wear out more quickly.

Choose a good quality cotton sateen for lining and make sure it is the best one available. A poor quality lining is a false economy as it will wear out long before the curtain fabric and necessitate relining. Lining sateen is available in various widths and colours, including natural and white. It is preferable, however, to use a neutral colour that blends well with most furnishing fabrics. It is then possible to have all the curtains in the house lined with the same colour lining, and this gives a much more pleasing effect from the outside of the house.

Cotton sateen is light in weight, and because it is not evenly woven it is not possible to pull a thread to straighten the edge. This means that each length should be cut either against a square table, or cut using a set square. Do not try to tear it.

A metal insulating lining can also be used which is completely draughtproof, and this makes it a particularly good choice when

making curtains for doors.

Interlinings

Interlined curtains have all the advantages of lined curtains. As well as helping the curtains to drape well, an interlining gives a luxurious padded look which shows off the texture or pattern of the fabric to the best advantage. It is particularly effective when more delicate furnishing fabrics are being used, such as satin, dupion or silk, as the interlining gives the fabric 'body'. Interlining is also an effective insulator and keeps out cold and draughts. It is placed between the curtain fabric and the lining.

Bump and domette are the fabrics most used for interlining curtains, although flannelette sheeting is also suitable. Bump is a thick, soft, fluffy fabric made from cotton waste; it is available bleached or unbleached and is usually 120 cm (48 in.) wide. Domette is similar in appearance but not quite so fluffy. Neither one is washable, so interlined curtains must be dry cleaned.

It is certainly well worth practising the technique of interlining curtains as the finished result is undoubtedly worth the extra time involved. These curtains are extremely costly if made professionally.

Measuring and estimating

When the curtain track and fittings have been chosen and fixed, it is possible to estimate the amount of fabric required. A track or decorative rod is usually placed 5-10 cm (2-4 in.) above the window frame. Remember to extend the track 15-46 cm (6-18 in.) at each side of the frame depending on the effect required, the width of the window and the thickness of the curtain fabric. Remember a wide window will need more room at each side of the frame to accommodate the curtains when drawn back.

Measure the window carefully and decide on the exact position of the track. Use a wooden meter stick or rigid rule to do this as accurate measurements cannot be obtained

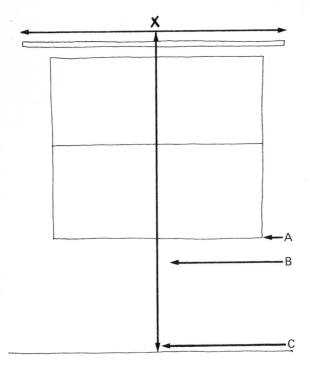

Fig. 101 **Deciding on the length of the curtains: (A) sill length; (B) below sill; (C) floor length; (X) position of track**

an allowance for turnings for hems and headings; allow 15-23 cm (6-9 in.) inclusive.

When using patterned fabric allow an extra pattern repeat on each 'drop' of curtain cut out. All curtains should finish at the same position of the pattern. Plan the curtains so that the pattern starts at the lower edge of the curtain after making allowance for the hem.

Fig. 102 **The same window treated in two different ways, showing the illusions of height and width**

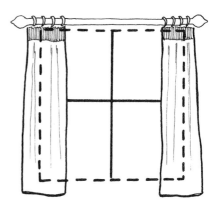

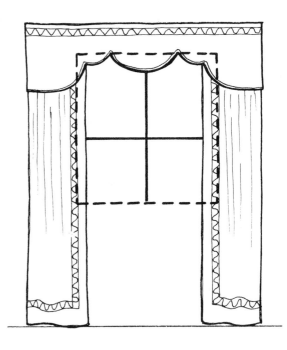

with a tape measure. Draw a diagram and mark in the appropriate measurements.

Decide where the curtains are to finish. If they are to hang to the sill, they should end 5-10 cm (2-4 in.) below the sill. If they are to hang to the floor they should finish within 1.3 cm (½ in.) of the floor or carpet (fig. 101). Avoid any inbetween measurement as the curtains will be out of proportion to the window. It is a common mistake to make the curtains hang too far below the sill and this spoils the finished crisp effect.

These are the two measurements necessary to estimate the amount of fabric required: (i) the width of the track (not the window) measured from end to end, and (ii) the finished length of the curtains, i.e. the 'drop', measured from the position from which the curtains will hang to the required bottom edge. To these measurements must be added

Decide how many widths of fabric will be required to give the necessary fullness to the curtains. This depends on the weight and thickness of the fabric chosen and the heading being used. Bear in mind that light unlined curtains need more fullness than heavy interlined ones. The following is a useful guide.

(1) Gathered headings require approximately one and half times the width of the track.

(2) Pinch pleats and box pleats require from two to two and a half times the width of the track.

(3) Pencil pleats and many of the commercial headings require from two and a half to three times the width of the track.

It is advisable to work out individual requirements carefully.

To obtain the required fullness it may be necessary to join widths or half widths together. If a half width has to be joined make sure that this is placed so that it comes at the outer edge of the curtain. Always err on the generous side when calculating the amount of fullness needed — nothing looks worse than curtains that are skimped. It is preferable to choose a less expensive fabric and use more, than to use an expensive fabric with too little fullness.

The same amount of fabric will be needed for the lining as for the curtains.

Cutting out the fabric

Whether making unlined, lined or interlined curtains, the rules for cutting out are the same.

(1) Place the fabric on a large square or rectangular table with the selvedge of the fabric running down the longest side. The end of the table can then be used to square up the fabric if necessary.

(2) Draw a thread if possible to get a straight line for cutting.

(3) Always cut plain fabric to the grain of the material. If a patterned fabric is badly printed and is not on the grain, always cut to the pattern and not to the grain.

(4) Cut out each length of curtain taking care to match patterns. Before cutting, measure and mark with pins or tailor's chalk. Use tailor's chalk and a meter stick to draw a straight line on the position of the cut. Remember to allow for pattern repeats and turnings and check these carefully before cutting.

(5) Mark the top of each length of curtain fabric as it is cut off the roll. This is particularly important when using plain fabric, velvet or velour. The pile on the velvet should run down the curtain length so that any dust can be easily removed from the curtains.

(6) Cut off all selvedges as these often make the seams pucker.

(7) When using patterned fabric cut off any wastage as the lengths are cut. If this is not done, confusion can arise when making up the curtains and matching the pattern repeats.

MAKING THE CURTAINS

When making curtains, whether they are unlined, lined or interlined, always prepare the side and bottom hems first. The curtains are then sized up to the required finished length and the heading applied.

Unlined curtains

(a) Cut out the curtains matching the patterns carefully. Cut off the selvedges. Where more than one width is necessary in each curtain, joins should be made using a run and fell seam (see page 27).

(b) For the side hems, fold and tack 1.3 cm (½ in.) double hems, ie. making the turning the same size as the hem (fig. 103). Machine stitch ensuring a firm edge to the curtain. The width of the hem can be varied to suit the fabric, e.g. if using a striped fabric make sure

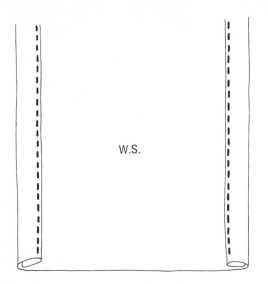

Fig. 103 **Making a 1.3 cm (½ in.) double hem at each side of an unlined curtain**

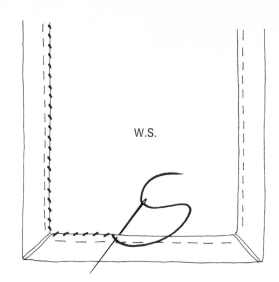

Fig. 105 **Serge stitching the two side hems and the lower hem on a lined curtain**

that this is folded to finish with a complete stripe or set of stripes.

(c) To make the bottom hem of the curtain, turn up 5 cm (2 in.) at the lower edge of the curtain, to make a 2.5 cm (1 in.) double hem (fig. 104). Tack. This hem can then be machine stitched, taking care to keep a neat finish on the right side of the curtain. For heavier fabrics the hems can be hand stitched.

(d) Make a heading or apply tape as required (see page 65).

Fig. 104 **Making a 2.5 cm (1 in.) double hem at the lower edge of an unlined curtain**

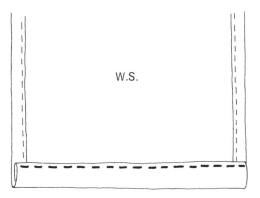

Lined curtains
Preparing the curtain
(a) Cut out the curtains matching patterns carefully. Cut off all selvedges.
(b) Widths or half widths should be joined with a plain seam (page 26) and pressed open. Do not neaten the edges.
(c) Turn in 3.8 cm (1½ in.) at the sides and lower edge of the curtain (fig. 105) and tack. Mitre the two lower corners (see page 37) and slipstitch. Using matching single thread serge stitch (see page 25) the two side hems and the lower hem (fig. 105).

Preparing the lining
(a) Cut the lining to the same size as the curtain fabric, cutting off all the selvedges.
(b) Join widths or half widths as necessary, using a plain seam (page 26). Press open. Half widths on the lining should match as closely as possible the half widths on the curtain fabric.

Applying the lining
(a) Lock the lining to the curtain fabric to ensure that it does not fall away and drop when the curtain is hanging.

'Locking' consists of a row of large loose stitches, made so that they do not pull and thereby pucker the curtain. It is worked two or three times in a width of 120 cm (48 in.) fabric. Use thread that matches the curtain fabric and not the lining. Match the seams of the lining to the seams of the curtain material if possible.

(b) Press the curtain carefully and place on a large table with the wrong side uppermost. Press the lining and place it on top of the curtain with wrong sides together, matching the seams of the lining to the seams of the curtain where possible. The raw edges of the lining should be flush with the curtain at the lower edge and an equal amount of lining should extend at each side of the curtain.

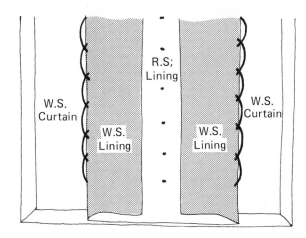

Fig. 107 **Lined curtain showing rows of tacking stitches**

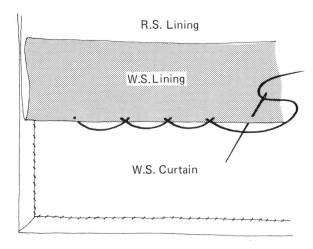

Fig. 106 **Working a row of locking stitches**

(c) Fold back the lining at the centre of the curtain and lock into position (fig. 106), making stitches every 10-15 cm (4-6 in.). Make another row of locking half way between the centre and both sides of the curtain (fig. 107).

(d) When the locking is complete any excess lining extending at the two sides of the curtain should be trimmed off so that the lining is flush with the curtain both at the two sides and at the bottom edge.

(e) Fold in the lining 2.5 cm (1 in.) at the sides and bottom edge, making sure that the corner of the lining meets the mitre on the curtain (fig. 108). Tack round the two sides and lower edge.

Fig. 108 **Tacking lining to the curtain and matching mitre**

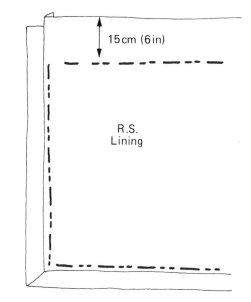

(f) Sew a line of tacking stitches across the curtain approximately 15 cm (6 in.) from the top edge. This keeps the lining firmly in position until the heading is worked.

(g) Slipstitch the lining to the curtain at the two sides and the lower edge (page 24) using matching thread, leaving the top 15 cm (6 in.) of the curtain un-stitched to allow for the heading to be finished.

(h) Make a heading, or apply tape as required (see page 65).

Detachable linings

As well as making curtains with conventional linings, it is also possible to make detachable linings using a special curtain lining tape. These linings are easily removed for washing or dry cleaning and can be changed from one set of curtains to another if required. The lining is made quite separately with its own tape and attached to the curtain by the same hooks which suspend the curtain from the track.

It is important to remember, however, that these detachable linings do not have the same professional finish as permanently lined curtains. They do not enhance the curtains in the same way because they are not locked and sewn to the curtain fabric and therefore they do not drape and hang so well.

(a) Make up unlined curtains as on page 59.

(b) Cut the lining to the same size as the curtain, but make the lining 2.5 cm (1 in.) shorter than the finished curtain measured from the bottom hem to the heading tape.

(c) Make up the lining by machining 2.5 cm (1 in.) double hems at the sides and bottom hem and leave the top edge unfinished.

(d) At one end of the lining tape pull out 3.8 cm (1½ in.) of cord and knot the ends. Cut off the surplus tape to within 0.6 cm (¼ in.) of the cord. Turn under the end of the tape and stitch across the fold to neaten and secure the knotted ends.

(e) With the right side of the lining facing, place the lining tape, cord side upper-most, between the two sides of the tape. Tack into position. Neaten the other end of the tape as above, but leave the cords free for gathering up the lining.

(f) Machine the lining tape into position along the top and bottom edges.

(g) Draw up the cords so that the lining matches the width of the curtain. Attach hooks first into the small hole in the top of the lining tape and then through to the pocket of the curtain heading tape and turn over in the usual way.

Interlined curtains

(a) Cut out the curtain and the lining as for lined curtains.

(b) Cut the interlining to the same size as the curtain fabric and join widths and half widths as necessary. As bump and domette tend to stretch, this should be done with a lapped seam, using two rows of zigzag machine stitching.

(c) Place the curtain fabric on a large table with the wrong side uppermost. Lay the interlining on the wrong side of the curtain, matching sides and lower edges. Fold back the interlining at the centre of the curtain and lockstitch into posi-tion, as for lined curtains (fig. 106), making three rows of locking stitches to every width of 120 cm (48 in.) fabric.

(d) When the locking is complete, fold over 5 cm (2 in.) at each side of the curtain and at the bottom edge, folding both the interlining and the curtain fabric to-gether. Mitre the two corners, cutting away the bump to make the mitre less bulky. Tack and herringbone-stitch the material into position to make a firm edge (fig. 109). Slipstitch the mitred corners.

(e) Place the lining on top of the inter-

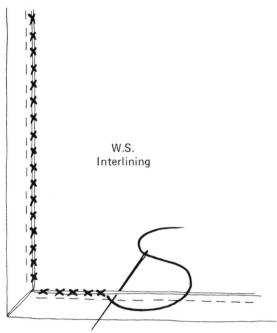

Fig. 109 **Stitching interlining to curtain using herring-bone stitch**

(a) When the interlining has been locked to the curtain, but before the two sides and bottom are turned over to make the hem, a 5-7.5 cm (2-3 in.) border of wadding is applied to the wrong side of the curtain. In order to cover the wadding a 7.5-9 cm (3-3½ in.) allowance must be made at the sides and bottom of the curtain and this must be allowed for at the bottom edge when cutting out the curtains. The wadding must then be prepared so that it fits into this allowance.

(b) Make a line of tacking stitches down the sides and bottom of the curtain to indicate the position of the fold of the hem. If braid is being applied to the finished curtains make another row of tacking stitches 12.5-15 cm (5-6 in.) in from the edge of the curtain (fig. 110).

(c) Prepare the wadding by cutting strips

lining right side up and work three rows of locking stitches as for lined curtains.

(f) Fold in the lining 3.8 cm (1½ in.) at the side and bottom edges of the curtain, matching mitres, and finish as for lined curtains.

(g) Make the heading or apply tape as required. In order to make the heading less bulky, the bump can be cut off to the required depth of the heading at the top edge of the curtain.

Making a wadded edge

When interlining curtains, a wadded edge can also be made. This produces a thick luxurious edge to the curtain and it is also often used in conjunction with a decorative braid on the outside of the curtain. Sheet wadding, either cotton or synthetic, is used to make this border, which should be applied to both side hems as well as to the bottom hem. This makes the curtains interchangeable. A wadded edge is most effective when used on floor length curtains.

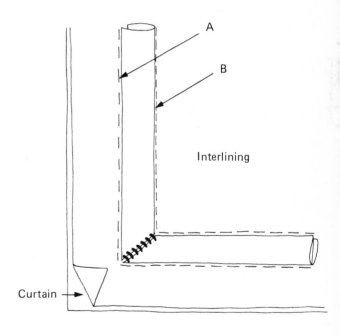

Fig. 110 **Wadding mitred and oversewn. Tacking line A shows position of finished edge of curtain. Tacking line B is used when applying braid to right side of curtain**

18 cm (7 in.) wide by the length required; fold into three lengthwise and tack. Mitre the corners by cutting and butting together. Oversew loosely to hold them into position (fig. 110).

(d) Fold over the side and bottom hems (both curtain and interlining) to cover the wadded edge. Mitre the corners and herringbone into position, then tack (fig. 111).

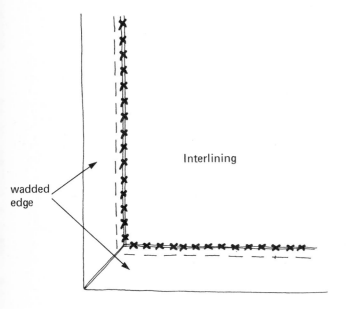

Fig. 111 **Wadded edge herringbone stitched in position**

(e) Finish the curtain by applying the lining as for lined curtains (page 60), but turning it to leave a 5-6.5 cm (2-2½ in.) border all round, and slipstitch.

(f) Make the heading and apply tape as required. Cut off the wadded edge at the top of the curtain to avoid extra bulk.

The width of the wadded edge depends to some extent on the fabric being used and the amount of fabric available as it slightly reduces the width of the curtain.

64

Applying decorative braid

A decorative braid can be applied to a curtain with or without a wadded edge. When a curtain has a wadded edge the braid should be stitched in position on a line to correspond with the finished width of the wad, i.e. 6.5-7.5 cm (2½ - 3 in.) from the edge of the finished curtain. The braid is sewn to the curtain before applying the lining and the heading.

(a) For a curtain without a wadded edge, tack a guide line 6.5-7.5 cm (2½ - 3 in.) in from the finished edge of the curtain at sides and bottom (fig. 112). For a curtain with a wadded edge it is easier to tack the guide line at the same time as making the wadded edge (see page 63).

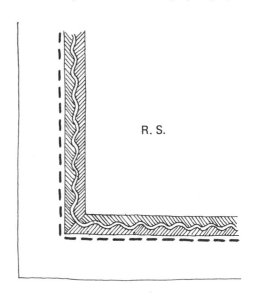

Fig. 112 **Guide line for application of braid to right side of curtain**

(b) Tack the braid to this guide line and backstitch into position sewing the outer edge first. Mitre the corners and stab stitch through to the interlining. Complete the backstitching on the inner edge of the braid. When applying braid, care must be taken to see that the stitches are not pulled too tightly. This can make the braid pucker, and a disappointing result will be obtained.

(c) Apply the lining and the heading to the curtain.

Applying decorative cord

Furnishing cord is made up of three or four thick cotton or silk strands twisted together, and is similar in appearance to piping cord. It has the advantage of being less expensive than most decorative braids. This cord can be applied to curtains in the same way as a decorative braid (page 64), or it can look most effective when applied to the edges of a curtain. As it needs to be firmly attached, but not too tightly, great care must be taken when applying it otherwise the finished effect will be spoiled. As it is sewn on to the very edge of the curtain it is not possible to tack it and therefore extra care is necessary in positioning it correctly.

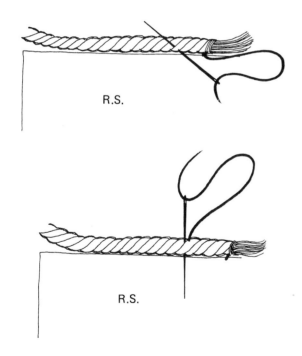

Figs. 113 and 114 **Applying decorative cord to a curtain**

(a) Before applying the cord, bind the end with thread to avoid it unravelling (fig. 113).

(b) With the right side of the curtain facing, place the cord onto the edge of the curtain, holding it with the left hand to control it.

(c) Using matching button thread pick up 3 mm (1/8 in.) on the fold of the curtain and insert the needle behind three strands of the cord. Take the needle back again into the fold of the curtain and continue stitching in this way (fig. 114). When reaching a corner, twist the cord slightly to enable a neat turn to be made. Before finishing off, tie the ends of the cord in two places and cut inbetween them. This avoids the cord unravelling too much.

(d) To finish off, take the cord to the wrong side of the curtain and insert under the lining. Unravel the cord and stitch down the strands neatly.

CURTAIN HEADINGS

The use of decorative curtain headings has become increasingly popular over recent years. Before the introduction of such a variety of commercially made heading tapes, it was necessary to make these decorative headings entirely by hand. Commercial tapes have greatly assisted people to successfully make their own pinch-pleated and pencil-pleated headings, as these tapes are quick and easy to apply. The hooks can easily be removed from the tape for washing or dry cleaning, whereas hand-made headings usually need to be dry cleaned because of their construction.

With the wide selection of tapes available it is usually possible to find one to suit a particular need. The pleating or gathering produced by these tapes is formed by inserting single, double or triple hooks into pockets on the tape. These hooks are made especially

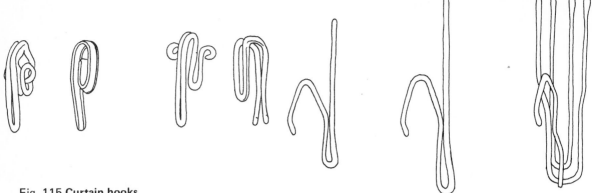

Fig. 115 **Curtain hooks**

for the purpose and can be bought separately (fig. 115).

Hand-made headings have the advantage of being made specifically to suit individual requirements, the pleating or gathering being made to complement the pattern of the fabric. They are also less expensive, as commercial heading tapes and hooks can add considerably to the cost of the curtains. They are, of course, more time consuming to work but for those who enjoy hand sewing their construction should present few problems.

Commercial headings

Gathered heading

This standard pocketed tape 2.5 cm (1 in.) wide produces a simple gathered heading suitable for use under pelmets or valances where the heading does not show. It can also be used on simple lined and unlined curtains when only a small frill is required above the heading. This tape can be obtained in cotton or man-made fibre for use with lighter fabrics or synthetics. Allow at least one and a half times the width of the track when calculating curtain fabric.

Applying tape without a frill

(a)   Measure the width of the curtain to obtain the amount of tape required. Use a wooden meter stick or rigid rule.

(b)   Size up the curtains by measuring from

the bottom edge of the curtain to obtain the correct position for the tape. Measurements should be taken every 30.5 cm (12 in.) along the curtain to obtain an accurate result. For a curtain without a frill the tape is sewn in position 3 mm (1/8 in) from the top edge of the curtain and any surplus fabric is turned in at the top of the curtain (fig. 116). These curtains can then be lengthened at a later date if necessary, by removing the heading tape and lengthening from the top edge This avoids a mark at the bottom hem.

Fig. 116 **Surplus fabric turned in at the top edge of the curtain to allow for ease in lengthening**

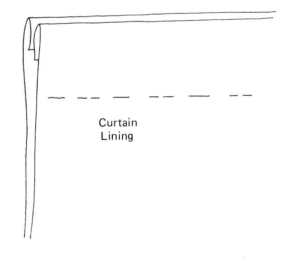

Curtain
Lining

(c) Cut the heading tape to the width of the curtain plus 2.5 cm (1 in.) for turnings at each end.

(d) Tack the heading tape into position at the top edge of the curtain, turning in 1.3 cm (½ in.) of tape at each end to neaten. Pull out the cords at each end and knot together.

(e) Machine along top and bottom edges of tape and along the two ends (fig. 117).

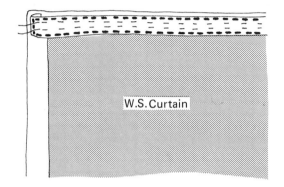

Fig. 117 **Heading machined into position**

When machining tapes to curtains always stitch along the top edge of the tape first. Take out of the machine and stitch the second line of stitching at the lower edge of the tape in the same direction. This prevents the heading from puckering, and produces a more even result.

(f) Insert the hooks into the tape and draw up the cords on the outside edge of the curtain to make a gathered heading of the required width. Do not cut off the surplus cord but tie neatly into a large bow or use a cord tidy for a neat finish. These cords can then be released easily for washing or dry cleaning.

Applying tape with a frill

(a) Measure the width of the curtain to obtain the amount of tape required.

(b) Size up the curtains to obtain the correct position for the tape, allowing 5-7.5 cm (2-3 in.) extra in length in order to make the frill.

(c) Tack the heading tape to the top edge of the curtain, covering the raw edges. Fold over onto the lining to the depth of the frill required approximately 2.5-3.8 cm (1-1½ in.). Pin, tack and machine stitch all round the tape, and finish as in fig. 118.

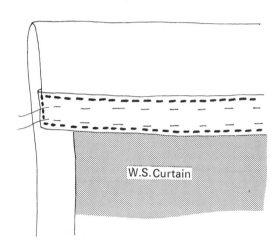

Fig. 118 **Application of tape for a curtain with a frill**

(d) If the fabric lacks body and tends to fall over at the top edge, a strip of stiffening, such as Vilene, tailor's canvas or buckram, could be inserted into the fold at the top of the curtain before the tape is applied.

Pinch-pleated heading

Attractive pinch pleats can be achieved by using one of the several tapes available. These tapes also stiffen the heading. With some tapes the pleats are formed automatically by drawing up the cords on the tape but with others it is necessary to reduce the width of the curtain by inserting the special pleating hooks in the tape. When using this tape, it is necessary to know the approximate width

67

down to which the fabric will pleat. The following table gives a rough guide, but if in doubt first pleat up the tape before applying it to the curtain, and work out the formula for the individual curtain. Use four-pronged hooks for making triple pleats (fig. 119), three-pronged hooks for making double pleats, and two-pronged hooks for making single pleats.

pinch pleat tapes are available in cotton and man-made fibres for use with synthetic or lighter fabrics. They vary in depth from 3.8-15 cm (1½-6 in).

Applying the tape The tape is sewn onto the curtains 3 mm (1/8 in.) from the top edge of the curtain, and is applied following the instructions given on page 67. Take care to follow the manufacturer's instructions to

	Single pleats	*Double pleats*	*Triple pleats*
120 cm (48 in.) fabric pleats down to:	66 cm (26 in.) using 9 hooks	61 cm (24 in.) using 7 hooks	58.5 cm (23 in.) using 5 hooks
183 cm (72 in.) fabric pleats down to:	100 cm (39 in.) using 14 hooks	96 cm (38 in.) using 10 hooks	82 cm (32 in.) using 8 hooks
245 cm (96 in.) fabric pleats down to:	135 cm (53 in.) using 19 hooks	127 cm (50 in.) using 14 hooks	109 cm (43 in.) using 11 hooks

These measurements allow 3.8 cm (1½ in.) for side hems, and approximately 2.5 cm (1 in.) for joining widths and half widths together. When calculating fabric remember that these tapes use two to two and a half times the width of the track. Most of the

ensure that the tape is applied with the pockets in their correct position.

Pencil-pleated heading

There are several different tapes available that produce pencil pleats. These are made in both cotton and man-made fibres, and vary in depth from 6.5 cm to 15 cm (2½ to 6 in.). The pencil pleats are all produced by drawing up cords on the tape, and require an amount of fabric two and a half to three times the width of the track (fig. 120).

Fig. 119 Deep pinch pleat heading: (i) using cords to automatically draw up the tape into pleats; (ii) using special pleater hooks to form the heading into pleats

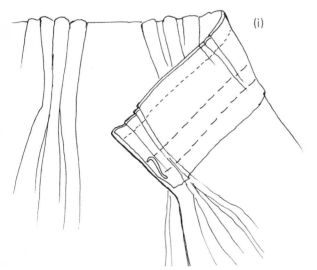

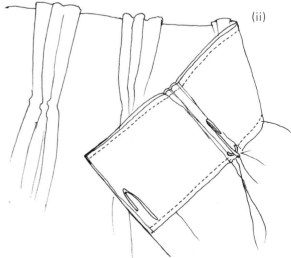

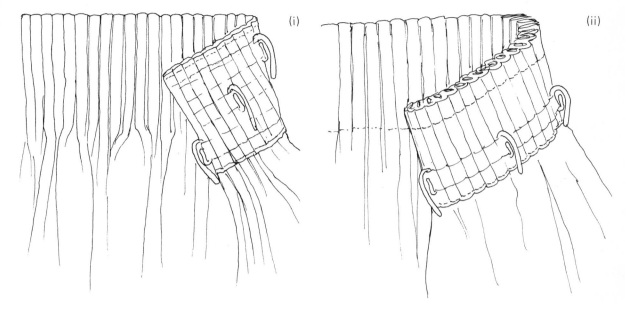

Fig. 120 **Pencil pleat heading tapes: (i) Rufflette Trident, a cotton/rayon tape producing inexpensive pencil pleats with staggered pockets to give three different suspension points (ii) Rufflette Regis, a cotton and nylon tape producing crisp pencil pleats**

Applying the tape These tapes are sewn onto the curtain 3 mm (1/8 in.) from the top edge of the curtain, and should be applied as on page 67. Follow the manufacturer's instructions to ensure that the tape is applied with the pockets in their correct position.

Hand-made headings

Great scope exists for those willing to spend a little time and imagination creating original headings for curtains and decorative valances. All the following headings can be adapted and adjusted to fit individual requirements for really professional results.

Stiffening the heading When using curtain fabric that lacks body it is often necessary to stiffen the heading to obtain a crisp effect. This can be done very easily if buckram or Vilene is used. Special buckram for this purpose is obtainable in various widths, but the most usual for a curtain heading is 10-15 cm (4-6 in.). The depth used will

depend on the length of the curtains and the individual window. As with non-woven interfacings, it is also possible to obtain special iron-on buckram, which is very simple to apply. These stiffenings should be tacked and ironed onto the top of the curtain in the correct position before the heading is worked (fig. 121).

Fig. 121 **Stiffening tacked into position at the top of the curtain**

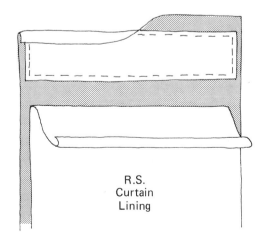

R.S.
Curtain
Lining

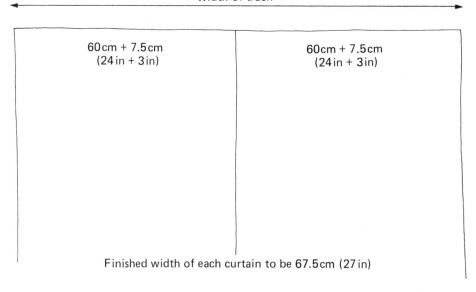

120 cm (48 in)
Width of track

60 cm + 7.5 cm
(24 in + 3 in)

60 cm + 7.5 cm
(24 in + 3 in)

Finished width of each curtain to be 67.5 cm (27 in)

Fig. 122 **Planning a gathered heading**

Simple gathered heading
The construction of the curtain is as for lined or unlined curtains (see pages **59** and **60**), but the heading is made to fit the window or track precisely. When calculating fabric for this heading allow one and a half to twice the width of the track to obtain the necessary fullness.

(a) Take the measurement of the track and divide it into two. Add 7.5 cm (3 in.) for each overlap of the curtain at the centre of the window. The heading is then gathered up to finish to this measurement (see example in fig. 122).

(b) Turn over the amount needed for the heading: 1.3 cm (½ in.) if under a pelmet; 5-6.5 cm (2-2½ in.) if a frill is required.

(c) Divide the width of the curtain into four equal sections and mark with tailor's chalk or pins. Gather each section separately with two rows of running stitches 3 mm (1/8 in.) apart (fig. 123).

(d) Cut a piece of plain heading tape the length of the finished heading plus 2.5 cm (1 in.) for turnings (fig. 124). Divide into four equal sections, turning in 1.3 cm (½ in.) at each end of the tape.

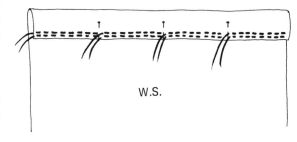

W.S.

Fig. 123 **Gathering four equal sections separately**

Fig. 124 **Marking out the heading tape and turning in 1.3 cm (½ in.) at each end**

70

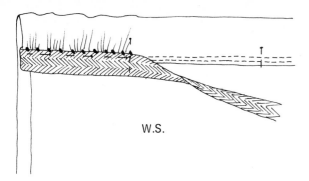

Fig. 125 **Applying the tape to the curtain, showing hemming along the top edge**

This tape is approximately 3.8 cm (1½ in.) wide, and looks rather like webbing.

(e) On the wrong side of the curtain pin the tape to the fabric matching tailor's chalk marks or pins, and gather up the curtain to fit into each section of the tape. Secure each section of gathering round a pin (fig. 125).

(f) Hem along the top edge of the tape picking up each gather separately, using strong thread or buttonhole thread for heavy curtains.

Fig. 126 **Curtain hooks sewn into position 6.5 cm - 7.5 cm (2½ in. - 3 in.) apart**

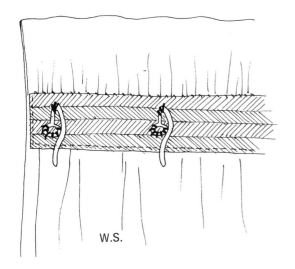

(g) Turn the curtain to the right side and adjust each gather along the lower edge of the heading tape. Stitch using a small backstitch between each gather.

(h) On the wrong side of the curtain sew hooks onto the tape using buttonhole stitch, securing at top and bottom edges, and using buttonhole thread for extra strength. Space the hooks 6.5 cm - 7.5 cm (2½-3 in.) apart, and sew them on 1.3 cm (½ in.) in from each end of the curtain (fig. 126).

Goblet-pleated heading

These are sometimes called french pleats. They make an extremely decorative heading. Goblet pleats can be used most successfully on fabrics with evenly-spaced patterns, since a part of the fabric design can be used to form the pleated heading.

When estimating the amount of fabric required, allow two to two and a half times the width of the track. The pleats are normally spaced 7.5-10 cm (3-4 in.) apart, and 10 cm (4 in.) is the usual amount allowed for each pleat. This measurement, however, may be altered when patterned fabric is being used to form the pleating.

(a) Prepare the curtains as for lined curtains (page 60).

(b) Take the measurement of the track and divide it into two. Add 7.5 cm (3 in.) for each overlap of the curtain at the centre of the window.

(c) To obtain the number of pleats needed for each curtain, measure the curtain exactly, and subtract the finished size of the heading from this measurement. Divide this measurement by ten to allow 10 cm (or by four to allow 4 in.) for each pleat, and the number of pleats will be obtained. If the measurement does not divide exactly by ten (or four) adjust the size of each pleat to take up the difference.

(d) As there must be a space at each end of the curtain there should be one more space than pleat. Divide the number of spaces by the finished heading measurement (in the following example, 50 cm or 20 in.), to give the size of the spaces (7.1 cm or 2¾ in. approximately). The pleat is formed inbetween this measurement (fig. 127).

(e) Stiffen the heading with 10 cm (4 in.) or 15 cm (6 in.) buckram to give impressive looking pleats.

(f) Turn in and press the top of the curtain and lining 2.5 cm (1 in.). Tack (fig. 128).

(g) Mark out pleats and spaces along the top edge of the curtain using tailor's chalk or pins (fig. 127).

The following example shows how to work out the number of pleats required for a curtain of 112 cm (44 in.).

Finished size of curtain	112 cm	(44 in.)
(less:) Finished size of heading -	50 cm	(20 in.)
Amount available for pleats	62 cm	(24 in.)

Number of pleats (i.e. divide by 10 (4))   6 pleats
Number of spaces (i.e. number of pleats + 1) 7 spaces

$$7)\overline{\,50\text{ cm (20 in.)}}$$
$$7.1\text{ cm (2¾ in.) approx.}$$

Therefore each space must measure 7.1 cm (2¾ in.) approx.

Fig. 127 **Planning goblet pleats**

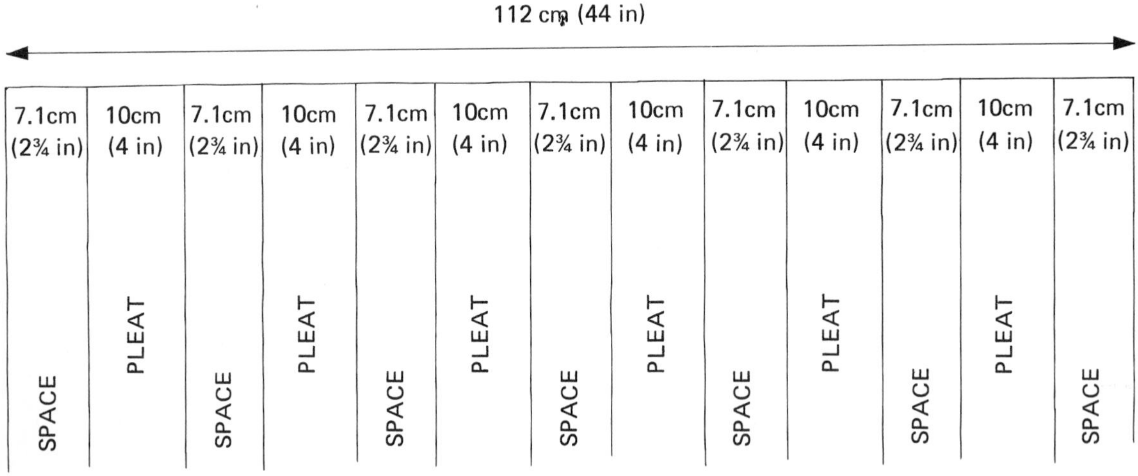

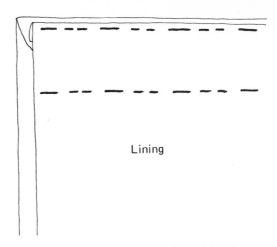

Fig. 128 **Preparation of heading for goblet pleats**

(h) Fold each pleat with wrong sides together (fig. 129). Tack and machine from the top of the curtain to the bottom of the stiffening (or the required depth of the heading) A-B, as in fig. 129. Divide this pleat into three small pleats and oversew the pleats together at point B (fig. 130). Stab stitch through the pleat to the back of the curtain and finish off.

(i) Open the pleats at the top of the curtain to make a goblet shape and oversew the pleating to the curtain 1.3 cm (½ in.) at each side of the machine stitching at

112 cm (44 in)

7.1cm (2¾ in)	10cm (4 in)	7.1cm (2¾ in)	10cm (4 in)	7.1cm (2¾ in)	10cm (4 in)	7.1cm (2¾ in)	10cm (4 in)	7.1cm (2¾ in)	10cm (4 in)	7.1cm (2¾ in)	10cm (4 in)	7.1cm (2¾ in)
SPACE	PLEAT	SPACE	PLEAT	SPACE	PLEAT	SPACE	PLEAT	SPACE	PLEAT	SPACE	PLEAT	SPACE

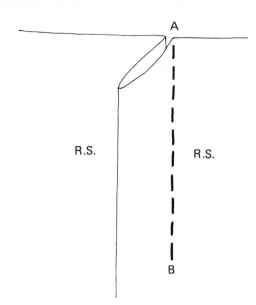

Fig. 129 Folding pleats with wrong sides together

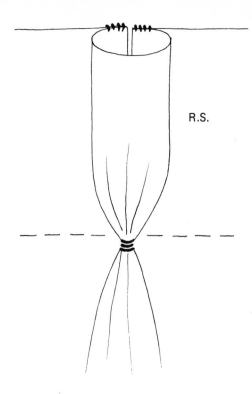

Fig. 131 Securing a goblet pleat at the top edge of the curtain

Fig. 132 Heading tape applied behind goblet pleats

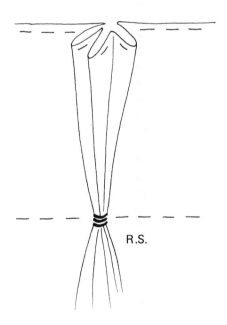

Fig. 130 Pleat divided into three

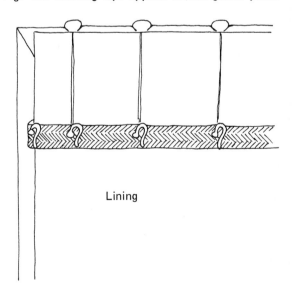

Lining

the centre (fig. 131).

(j) Fill the opening of the goblet pleat with cotton wool or tissue paper. If a stiffening has not been used for the heading, fill the goblet with a circle of card to hold the pleat firm.

(k) On the wrong side of the curtain apply the heading tape as for the gathered heading (page 71) and sew on hooks to the tape behind each pleat, and 2.5 cm (1 in.) from each side of the curtain (fig. 132).

This heading can also be made into triple pleating by increasing the allowance made for the pleat to 15 cm (6 in.) instead of 10 cm (4 in.). This gives three larger pleats which are not opened at the top as for the goblet pleat, but are secured at the top of the curtain with a few oversewing stitches (fig. 133).

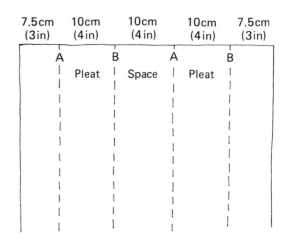

7.5cm (3in)	10cm (4in)	10cm (4in)	10cm (4in)	7.5cm (3in)
A	B	A	B	
Pleat	Space	Pleat		

Fig. 134 **Marking out for a box-pleated heading**

(½ in.) should be turned in both of curtain and lining.

(b) Measure out and mark for pleating as in fig. 134, and allow 7.5 cm (3 in.) at each side of the curtain, with 10 cm (4 in.) spaces, to produce a heading with 5 cm (2 in.) box pleats and 5 cm (2 in.) spaces between. The depth of pleating is approximately 7.5 cm (3 in.). (These measurements can of course be varied in proportion.)

Fig. 135 **Folding fabric to make box pleats**

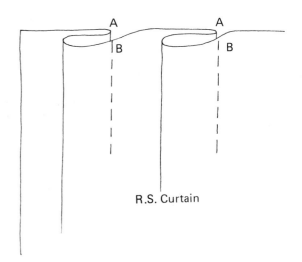

R.S. Curtain

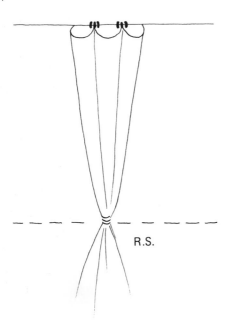

R.S.

Fig. 133 **Making triple pleating**

Box-pleated heading

This is a decorative heading which can be used most effectively on lined or unlined valances as well as on curtains. Allow approximately three times the finished width for this heading.

(a) Turn over 5 cm (2 in.) at the top of the curtain if unlined. If lined, 1.3 cm

74

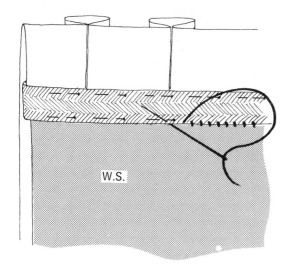

Fig. 136 Applying tape to box-pleated heading

(f) To hold each pleat in position, make a buttonhole bar on the wrong side of the curtain or valance at the bottom hem (fig. 138).

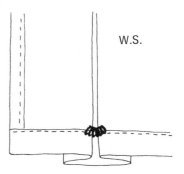

Fig. 138 A buttonhole bar made to hold the pleat in position

(c) Fold pleats with wrong sides together, matching marks A-B (fig. 135). Pin, tack and machine.
(d) Apply the heading tape to the wrong side of the curtain, hemming all round (fig. 136).
(e) Fold and form pleats on the right side of the curtain, securing them on the right side with a few oversewing stitches (fig. 137). Press.

(g) Sew hooks onto the heading tape in the usual way, 1.3 cm (½ in.) in from each end and behind each pleat.

Pencil-pleated heading

This is a gathered heading which involves using evenly spaced stitches. Instead of using small stitches as in the simple gathered heading, larger stitches are used on the wrong side of the curtain, with smaller ones on the right side. When the gathers are drawn up, large pencil pleats are formed on the right side.

(a) Allow three times the finished width of the curtain for this type of heading.
(b) Stiffen the heading with buckram or Vilene if necessary.
(c) Cut the heading tape to the required finished measurement.
(d) Fold in the top of the curtain and the lining 2.5 cm (1 in.).
(e) At the top and bottom edges of the heading or stiffening, draw two horizontal guide lines with tailor's chalk. Also make vertical guide lines 2 cm (7/8 in.) apart so that the stitches match up and are exactly opposite each other (fig. 139).

Fig. 137 Forming box pleats on the right side of the curtain

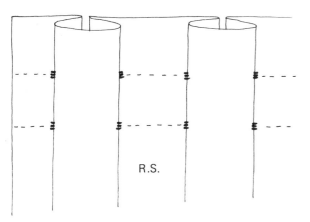

(f) Make a row of stitching along each guide line making 1.5 cm (5/8 in.) stitches on the wrong side of the curtain and 0.6 cm (¼ in.) stitches on the right side of the curtain (fig. 139).

(g) Pull up the gathering threads, adjusting the pleats to the length of the heading tape.

(h) Sew on the heading tape to the wrong side of the curtain, hemming along the top edge (fig. 140), and sewing in each pleat separately. Turn to the right side of the curtain and stitch the bottom edge of the tape to the curtain, using a small backstitch between each pleat (fig. 141). Sew hooks onto the tape.

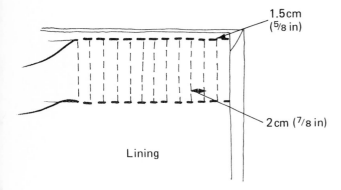

Fig. 139 **Horizontal and vertical guide lines marked before stitching**

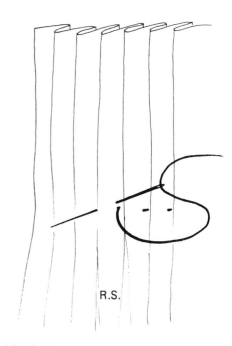

Fig. 141 **Making a backstitch between each pleat**

(i) To hold the pleating firm, make a lock stitch along the top edge of the curtain (fig. 142). Another row of lock stitching can be worked if the heading is very deep.

This type of pleating also looks effective if arranged in groups along the top of the curtain. The pleating can be adjusted in size by altering the length of the gathering stitch.

Smocked heading

A commercial 'smocked' heading tape is available which is most attractive when used on curtain headings and valances. It is also

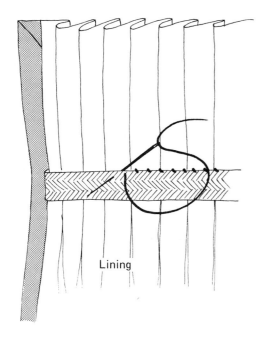

Fig. 140 **Hemming heading tape to wrong side of curtain**

76

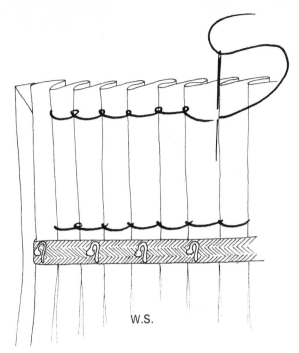

Fig. 142 **Locking the pleating into position**

possible to make a hand-made smocked heading using a honeycomb stitch. Allow approximately three times the width of the curtain for this heading. Other decorative smocking stitches could be used instead of honeycombing, and this heading gives great scope for those who enjoy handsewing.

Fig. 143 **Marking out a smocked heading**

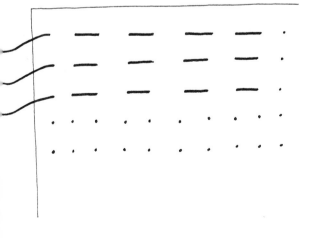

(a) Cut the heading tape to the required length.
(b) The smocking is formed by rows of even gathers, and it is essential that these gathers are evenly worked. To do this, make five horizontal lines of dots along the position for the heading (fig. 143), making sure that each is exactly below the one above. Sheets of dots for smocking can be obtained from craft and needlework shops, but they can also be marked out by hand. If a checked fabric such as gingham is used, the checks can be used as guides. The length of each stitch depends to some extent on the fabric being used, but for a curtain or a valance they should not usually be less than 1.3 cm (½ in.), as the effect would be lost if the gathering stitch were too small.
(c) Gather each row of dots and draw up firmly to straighten each fold (fig. 144). Secure the ends of the gathering thread round a pin.
(d) Starting at the second row of gathering stitches, and working on the right side of the curtain from left to right, pick up

Fig. 144 **Working a honeycombing stitch**

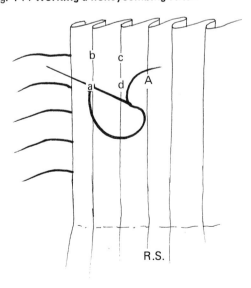

77

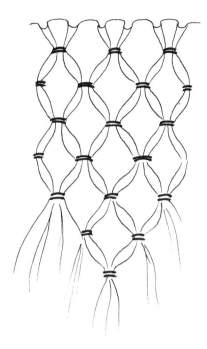

Fig. 145 **Honeycombing stitch**

(a) Cut a piece of curtain lining from selvedge to selvedge, and 1.3 cm (½ in.) larger all round than the finished length of the heading tape.

(b) Before applying the tape to the curtain, turn in the tape 1.3 cm (½ in.) at each end, and tack and machine stitch the wrong side of the lining strip to the tape (fig. 146).

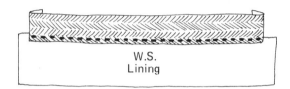

W.S.
Lining

Fig. 146 **Tape stitched to lining strip**

and work one stitch at a, which is the first pleat. Take up the thread to b and make another stitch. With the thread above the needle make another stitch at c, which is the second pleat. Keeping the thread above the needle, pick up another stitch at d. With the thread below the needle take up a stitch at A. This is the beginning of the next group of stitches (fig. 144).

(e) Continue along these two rows and work the next rows in the same way.

(f) When the honeycomb stitching is completed take out the gathering threads (fig. 145).

(g) Sew on the heading tape to the wrong side of the curtain as for a gathered heading (page 71), adjusting the smocking to fit. Sew on the hooks.

Covering the heading tape

On lined curtains with hand-made headings, a neat finish can be obtained on the wrong side of the curtain by covering the heading tape with a strip of the curtain lining fabric.

(c) Apply the heading tape to the wrong side of the curtain, and sew the hooks onto the tape.

(d) Fold up the lining strip to cover the tape, and slipstitch along the top edge of the tape under the shank of the hook (fig. 147).

Scalloped heading

This heading is often used on café curtains, but can also be used for valances or full length curtains. Make sure that the fabric used is firm. To make an unlined curtain with a scalloped heading follow the method below.

a) Prepare the curtain as on page 59.

(b) Allow approximately one and a half times the width of the track for this heading. Less fullness is necessary for this heading in order to show up the shaped top to advantage. Fabrics lacking body are, therefore, not recommended.

(c) To work out the scallops, prepare a pattern by cutting a piece of paper the width of the curtain and approximately 30.5 cm (12 in.) deep. Draw a straight line across the paper 10 cm (4 in.) from the top edge, and fold the paper in half.

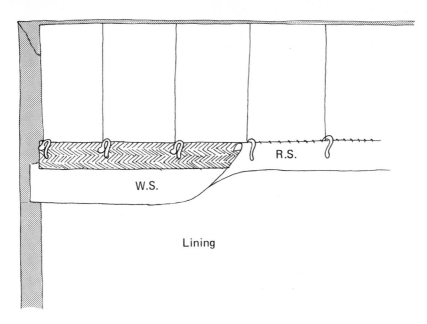

Fig. 147 **Covering the heading tape with a lining strip**

(d) Draw a scallop at the fold line at the centre of the paper and continue drawing scallops along the guide line working outwards to the side of the paper. Use a plate or compass for this and leave 3.8 cm (1½ in.) between each scallop. Leave at least 3.8 cm (1½ in.) at each end of the curtain (fig. 148). The number of scallops and their size will vary according to the width of the curtain and the size of the scallop, and adjustments will probably need to be made. When the scallops have been worked out satisfactorily, cut out the paper pattern.

(e) With the right side of the curtain facing, fold over the top of the curtain to the depth of the scallop, plus 7.5 cm (3 in.) for a hem allowance. Tack (fig. 149).

Fig. 148 **Planning a scalloped edge**

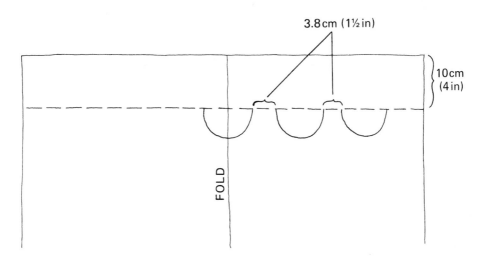

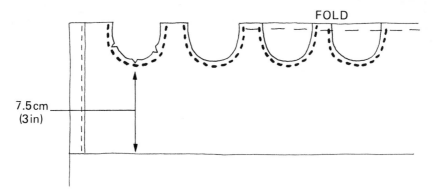

FOLD

7.5 cm
(3 in)

Fig. 149 **Making a scalloped heading**

(f) Place the paper pattern to the folded edge and mark round the scallops using tailor's chalk. Remove the pattern. Tack and machine stitch on the marking line and cut out scallops 0.6 cm (¼ in.) from the stitching line. Clip curves (fig. 149).

(g) Turn the facing over to the wrong side of the curtain and press well.

(h) Finish the lower edge of the facing with a 1.3 cm (½ in.) hem and slipstitch (fig. 150).

Fig. 150 **Slipstitching the lower edge of the facing on a scalloped heading**

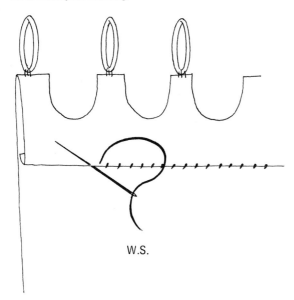

W.S.

(i) Sew rings onto the top of each scallop using buttonhole thread, then suspend the rings from the curtain rod (fig. 151).

Fig. 151 **Scalloped headings suspended (i) direct from the rod (ii) by rings**

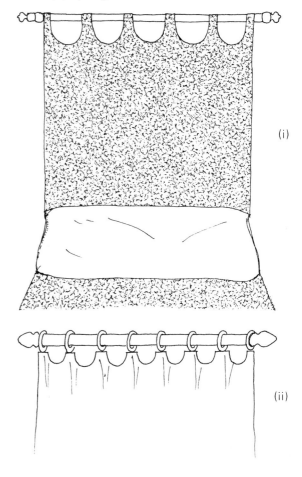

(i)

(ii)

Tab heading

This is a heading mostly used for café curtains, but it can also be used as a decorative heading when hanging a curtain or cushion on a pole at a bed head. The following instructions are for making an unlined curtain with a tab heading.

(a) Prepare the curtain as on page 59 but tack a 1.3 cm (½ in.) double hem at the top edge.

(b) Work out the number of tabs needed and mark their positions. Measure round the pole to obtain the overall length needed for the tab.

(c) For a tab 6.5 cm (2½ in.) wide (finished) and 23 cm (9 in.) long (finished), cut a strip of fabric 15 cm (6 in.) wide and 25.5 cm (10 in.) long. This allows 1.3 cm (½ in.) turnings. Fold the strip in half lengthwise, with right sides together, and tack and machine with 1.3 cm (½ in.) turnings. Leave the ends open (fig. 152).

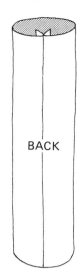

Fig. 153 **A tab, showing the seam at centre back**

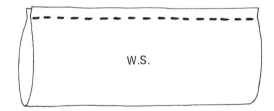

Fig. 152 **Making a tab**

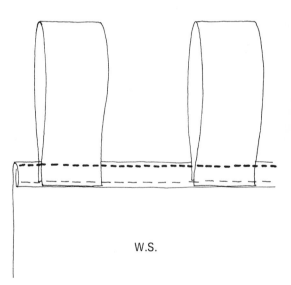

Fig. 154 **Stitching the tabs in position**

Fig. 155 **A tab heading suspended from a wooden rod**

(d) Turn the strip to the right side and press keeping the seam in the centre of the strip on the back of the tab (fig 153). Turn in the raw edges of the strip 1.3 cm (½ in.) and press.

(e) Apply the tabs to the wrong side of the curtain, tacking carefully into the marked positions. On the right side of the curtain, machine stitch 0.6 cm (¼ in.) all along the top edge of the curtain (fig. 154). Suspend the loops from the curtain rod (fig. 155).

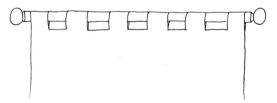

CAFE CURTAINS

These consist of two small pairs of curtains, one for the bottom half of the window and one for the top, the lower pair being suspended half way up the window. These curtains are versatile, and particularly useful in kitchens and bathrooms, or when an ugly view needs to be screened. They can be used very successfully with roller blinds and with pelmets, and can be adapted in many ways.

Café curtains are constructed in the same way as lined and unlined curtains, and any of the commercial or hand-made headings mentioned on the previous pages can be used.

SHOWER CURTAINS

These can be constructed in the same way as unlined curtains, and detachable linings can be made using special shower-curtain material. Alternatively the lining can be hung separately onto a rod made especially for the purpose.

CURTAIN TIE-BACKS

A simple tie-back can add considerably to the charm of a pair of curtains. They are quick and easy to make and are much less costly than commercial cord and tassel tie-backs.

Straight tie-back
This is made from a straight piece of fabric and can be stiffened with an interlining of Vilene, tailor's canvas, buckram, or pelmet buckram, depending on the stiffness required. Tie-backs can be finished with decorative braid, piping cord, fringing or other trimming if desired.
(a) Decide on the length and width of the tie-back. To estimate for length, take a piece of string or a tape measure round the curtain to obtain the required effect.

Beware of making the tie-back too short as this can cause the curtain to crease.
(b) From this measurement cut a strip of fabric, interlining and lining sateen the required length by the required width. Add 1.3 cm (½ in.) for turnings all round on the piece of face fabric and the lining sateen. Cut the ends of the strips into points or curves as desired (fig. 156).

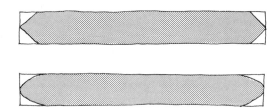

Fig. 156 **Cutting out a tie-back**

(c) Place the interlining on the wrong side of the fabric. Turn over 1.3 cm (½ in.) all round and herringbone stitch into position, mitring each end (fig. 157).

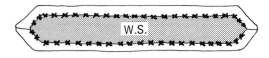

Fig. 157 **Stitching the interlining into position with a herringbone stitch**

(d) Turn under the edges of the lining sateen so that they finish 0.6 cm (¼ in.) from the edge of the tie-back. Slip-stitch into position (fig. 158).

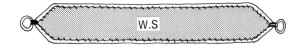

Fig. 158 **Tie-back showing lining slipstitched into position**

82

(e) Sew a brass or strong plastic curtain ring to each end of the tie-back, using buttonhole stitch and strong thread (fig. 158).

Shaped tie-back

In order to obtain a satisfactory shape for a tie-back (fig. 159), it is advisable to experiment first with a paper pattern.

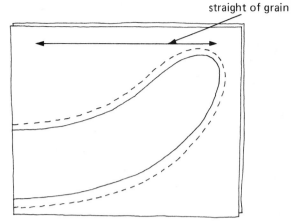

Fig. 160 **Cutting out a shaped tie-back allowing 1.3 cm (½ in) turnings**

(a) Decide on the approximate length of the tie-back, and cut out a curved strip of paper to represent it. Adjust this pattern until a pleasing effect is obtained.

(b) Fold and cut the final pattern in half and use one side only to cut out the fabric. Place the paper pattern to the fold of the fabric and cut out allowing 1.3 cm (½ in.) turnings all round (fig. 100). Cut out the lining sateen in the same way. Cut the interlining or buckram to the same size as the paper pattern, do not allow for turnings.

(c) The shaped tie-back is constructed in the same way as the straight tie-back, but care must be taken to clip any curves.

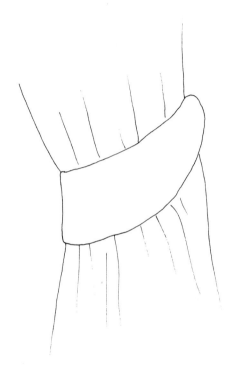

Fig. 159 **Shaped tie-back**

7·Pelmets and Valances

Pelmets and valances are used to create a decorative finish to the top of curtains.

Fig. 161 **Ideas for pelmets**

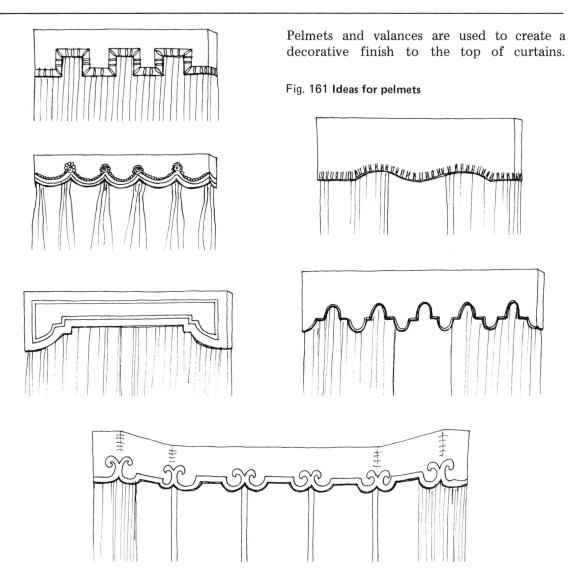

They also conceal the curtain rail and fittings and their design adds considerably to the decor of a room. Pelmets and valances can be formal or frivolous, decorated or plain (fig. 161). A simple design can be as effective as an ornate one, and care should be taken to suit the design to the fabric; advantage can also be taken of any idea or design that is suggested by the pattern. Pelmets and valances can also be used to change the 'shape' of a window by fixing them either lower or higher than the window frame, or extending them at each side. They also look most effective when used with roller blinds or café curtains, or with draped dressing tables.

PELMETS

Pelmets are economical to make at home and can considerably reduce the cost of curtaining a window, since only a simple gathered heading is necessary under a pelmet. The gathered heading requires less fullness than other decorative headings, and therefore less curtain fabric.

A pelmet is usually made from the same fabric as the curtains and is mounted onto a special buckram foundation. Pelmet buckram is golden brown in colour and consists of a coarse canvas impregnated with glue. It is sold by the metre, and is usually 90 cm (36 in.) wide, but it is possible to obtain it in narrower widths. This is preferable as joins do not then need to be made in the buckram to obtain the required length.

A pelmet stiffened with buckram is best fixed to a pelmet board and not to a valance rail. The valance rail is suitable only for valances made from lighter fabrics. A pelmet board should be approximately 10 cm (4 in.) deep by 1.5 cm (5/8 in.) thick and should extend 5-7.5 cm (2-3 in.) beyond the end of the curtain rail. It is fixed like a shelf, using brackets. The height of fixing above the window frame varies as this measurement is determined by the effect required. For

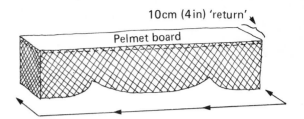

Fig. 162 **Plan of a pelmet showing 10 cm (4 in.) return at each end of the pelmet board**

an average window the board is fixed approximately 5-7.5 cm (2-3 in.) above the frame. The pelmet is then attached to the front edge of the board with drawing pins (fig. 162).

Pelmets made with buckram cannot be washed and should be dry cleaned only, but regular brushing will keep them in good condition.

Estimating the fabric
Measure the length of the pelmet board from wall to wall, remembering to include the 10 cm (4 in.) return at each end (fig. 162). To this measurement add 5 cm (2 in.) for turnings.

The depth of the pelmet is determined by the design, but as a rough guide allow 3.8 cm (1½ in.) pelmet depth to 30.5 cm (12 in.) of curtain drop, or one sixth of the total depth of floor length curtains. This gives a pelmet in proportion to the curtains. To this measurement add 10 cm (4 in.) for turnings. Pelmets do not usually look effective if made less than 18 cm (7 in.) deep. However, in rooms with low ceilings, keep the depth to a minimum in order to allow the maximum amount of daylight into the room.

Fig. 163 **The 120 cm (48 in.) width of fabric placed at centre of pelmet**

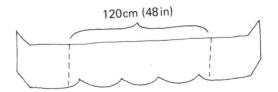

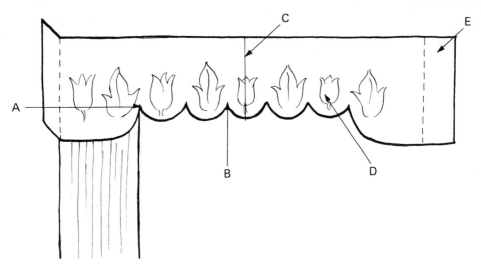

When using 120 cm (48 in.) wide fabric it is necessary to centre one width of fabric in the middle of the pelmet (fig. 163). Any extra fabric should be added to each side of this width. Never have a seam at the centre of the pelmet. When estimating the amount of fabric required, remember that patterns must match accurately.

The same amount of lining sateen and interlining is needed as for the face fabric. The use of interlining is particularly recommended when using a fabric that is light in weight, as it gives the fabric more body and the pelmet a slightly padded look.

Designing the pelmet

(a) Draw a rough sketch of the design required, bearing in mind the following essentials (fig. 164). The point where the curtains will hang when drawn back gives the measurement of the 'end' sections. The return at each end must be the same depth as the 'end' sections. The measurement of the pattern, or motif if a scallop is being made, must be considered; the motif can then be fitted in satisfactorily. The shallowest part of the pelmet must not allow the rail to show when the curtains are drawn back.

(b) Make a mark at the centre of the pelmet, then cut a pattern in brown paper or

Fig. 164 **Pelmet plan showing: (A) point where curtains hang; (B) narrowest part of pelmet; (c) centre of pelmet; (D) measurement of motif; (E) return at end of pelmet**

newspaper — strips can be pinned together — to the full size of the pelmet. Mark out the critical measurements described above, and start designing the pelmet from the centre, using plates or trays to draw round as guides. Use the first perfect curve as a template for the others. Pin the pattern up onto the board using drawing pins and adjust one side of the pattern only until a satisfactory effect is achieved. It is sometimes advisable to live with the paper pattern for a few days before the final pattern is cut!

(c) When a satisfactory design has been achieved, fold the pattern in half and cut the other side to match. The design is then ready to transfer to the buckram.

(d) If in doubt about a design, keep it simple — or straight. A simple pelmet can be decorated with a fringe, piping cord, tassels or other decorative trimmings, and this is far better than having an ornate design that has been badly planned.

Cutting the buckram

(a) Prepare the buckram by cutting a long strip the exact length of the pelmet, not forgetting to include the 10 cm (4 in.) returns at each end. If possible, avoid making joins in the buckram, but if this is necessary, join by overlapping 1.3 cm (½ in.) and machining into position.

(b) Lay the paper pattern onto the buckram and secure firmly in position. As the buckram is impregnated with glue, this can be done by damping the buckram very slightly and ironing the pattern to it. Cut out the buckram carefully, using a sharp pair of scissors.

Preparing the face fabric

Prepare a strip of fabric 10 cm (4 in.) longer than the exact size of the finished pelmet. The width of this strip must be 10 cm (4 in.) more than the greatest depth of the pelmet. This allows for the face fabric to be turned over onto the buckram (fig. 165). Join widths of fabric where necessary, remembering to keep a full width at the centre of the pelmet. Join the fabric with 1 3 cm (½ in.) seams, matching patterns carefully. Press seams open.

Applying the interlining

(a) Prepare a strip of bump or domette 5 cm (2 in.) wider than the exact size of the finished pelmet, joining the pieces

as on page 62.

(b) Place the buckram onto the interlining exactly in the centre. Starting at the top edge of the pelmet damp the buckram slightly with a small cloth at the edges. Fold over the interlining and press firmly onto the buckram with a hot iron (fig. 166). Continue in this way all round the pelmet, slashing concave curves and cutting away the surplus fabric on the convex curves. Right-angled turns also need slashing, and the surplus fabric should be trimmed away.

Applying the face fabric

Lay the buckram and the interlining onto the face fabric, checking that any patterns are placed correctly. Starting at the top edge, fold over the fabric onto the buckram as for the interlining. This fabric will have enough turnings to extend 2.5 cm (1 in.) beyond the interlining. Damp the buckram and press down in the same way, mitring the corners and cutting away surplus fabric. Slipstitch the corners. If the fabric frays easily, reinforce each slash made with a few buttonhole stitches (fig. 167).

Applying the trimming

Any decorative trimming should be stitched to the pelmet before the lining is applied. With the right side of the pelmet facing, stitch on the trimming using matching thread. Stabstitch through the buckram to the wrong side of the pelmet, taking care to keep a good line (fig. 168).

Fig. 165 **Preparing the face fabric for a pelmet**

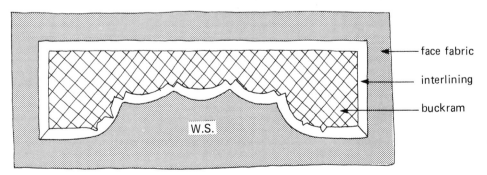

face fabric

interlining

buckram

W.S.

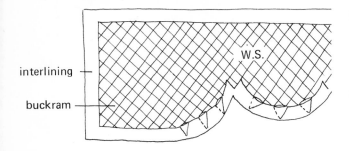

Fig. 166 **Application of interlining to pelmet**

Cord or braid can be used effectively to decorate the face of a pelmet.

Applying the lining and heading tape

(a)   Prepare a strip of lining sateen 5 cm (2 in.) deeper than the finished pelmet. Join the strips together if necessary with 1.3 cm (½ in.) turnings and press open.

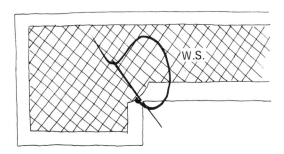

Fig. 167 **Reinforcing a slash with buttonhole stitches**

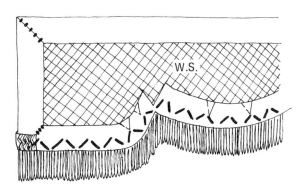

Fig. 168 **Trimming applied to pelmet with stab stitch**

88

(b)   With the wrong side of the pelmet facing, turn in the lining 1.3 cm (½ in.) and pin 0.6 cm (¼ in.) from the top edge of the pelmet. Turn in the sides in the same way.

(c)   Cut the lining to the shaped edge allowing 2.5 cm (1 in.) for turnings and turn in, slashing where necessary. Slipstitch the lining to the pelmet all round (fig. 169).

(d)   Pin a piece of 2.5 cm (1 in.) − 3.8 cm (1½ in.) heading tape along the top edge of the pelmet turning in 1.3 cm (½ in.) at each end. If possible match the tape to the colour of the lining.

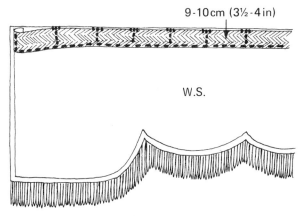

Fig. 169 **Heading tape applied to wrong side of pelmet**

(e)   Using matching buttonhole thread and a strong needle, backstitch the ends and lower edge of the tape to the pelmet, making sure that the stitches go through to the buckram but not to the face fabric. Stitch the tape down every 9-10 cm (3½-4 in.) to form pockets (fig. 169). Place a drawing pin in each pocket and attach to the pelmet board.

VALANCES

A valance can be made instead of a pelmet when a less firm fabric is being used, and a

rooms, kitchens and bathrooms where crisp cottons or ginghams are used. They are made exactly the same as lined or unlined curtains, and can be finished with any of the commercial heading tapes or hand-made headings.

softer, more informal effect is required (fig. 170).

Valances are not stiffened with buckram but are usually lined as for curtains. They are finished with a curtain heading tape and hung from a valance rail or attached to a pelmet board with drawing pins. The depth of a valance is calculated as for a pelmet. Valances are particularly suitable for bed-

Fig. 170 **Some ideas for valances**

8-Roller Blinds

Roller blinds are becoming increasingly popular and are easy and inexpensive to make at home. They are very attractive when used in kitchens and bathrooms and in many cases are much more practical than curtains. Roller blind kits are obtainable from large stores and do-it-yourself shops.

Holland is the best choice of fabric for a roller blind. It is available in a good range of patterns and plain colours and is ideally suited as it does not fray at the edges. It also repels dirt and dust and can be sponged clean. Holland is made in wide widths, so that joining is often unnecessary.

A PVC or plastic coated fabric can also be used and is particularly suitable for blinds in kitchens where cleaning becomes necessary more often.

Closely woven cottons, linens and some man-made fabrics are also suitable if small blinds are being made. These need to be sprayed first with a fabric stiffener. Avoid fabrics that are loosely woven or too thick. Large blinds made from these fabrics are not always successful as they do not roll well.

Make the roller blind from one width of fabric if possible. For a wide window the fabric can be used sideways if a plain fabric is used. Seams in a blind are not satisfactory as they stop the roller from working smoothly. With professionally stiffened fabrics that do not fray, it is not necessary to have side hems either, as this also adds bulk to the blind. However, if a do-it-yourself fabric stiffener is used, it is necessary to turn in the side hems 1.3 cm (½ in.) and machine into position using a zigzag stitch (or two rows of straight stitch placed close together). The fabric should then be pressed well. When machining, keep the fabric as flat as possible, as stiffened fabric can crack if folded.

The lower edge of the blind can be finished in numerous ways. A shaped edge can be made and applied to the bottom edge, or a decorative braid or fringe can be used to create an original design (fig. 171). Pull cords can be obtained in various styles, and a hand-made knotted or plaited cord could be made by the macramé enthusiast.

MEASURING THE WINDOW

Before buying the roller blind kit, it is important to decide whether the blind is to be fixed inside or outside the window recess. If a kit cannot be obtained in the exact size, buy the next size up and trim the roller down to the size required.

A roller blind kit consists of a wooden roller which has a spring and a metal end cap with a rectangular pin at one end of the roller. Another metal end cap with a round pin is provided to fit onto the other end of the roller when it has been cut to the exact size required. Two metal brackets are supplied; one is fixed to the left hand side of the window to take the sprung end and rectangular

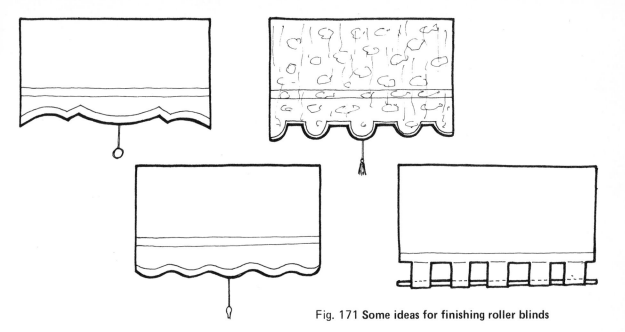

Fig. 171 **Some ideas for finishing roller blinds**

pin, and the other bracket is fixed at the right hand side of the window, and takes the end with the round pin (fig. 172). Follow the manufacturer's instructions for fixing these. Special tacks are also provided for applying the fabric to the roller. An acorn fitment with tacks and a pull cord is also provided, together with a wooden lath to give weight to the bottom hem of the blind.

MAKING THE ROLLER BLIND

(a) Cut the wooden roller to the correct size to fit between the two brackets.
(b) Cut the fabric to the exact size of the roller. If hems need to be made at each side, a 2.5 cm (1 in.) allowance must be

Fig. 172 **Fixing brackets for a roller blind**

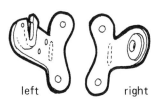

left   right

made for these. The length of the fabric should be approximately 15 cm (6 in.) longer than the measurement of the window. This allows for turnings at the bottom edge of the blind and also allows for surplus fabric round the roller when it is pulled down. Care must be taken to ensure that the fabric is cut accurately to the grain, otherwise the blind will not roll evenly. Square up the fabric with the edge of a table, or use a large set square when cutting.

(c) At the bottom edge turn up 1.3 cm (½ in.) to the wrong side of the blind and then turn over 3.8 cm (1½ in.) to

Fig. 173 **Making a hem along the lower edge of a roller blind using a zigzag stitch**

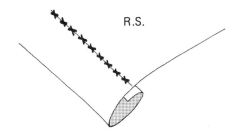

R.S.

91

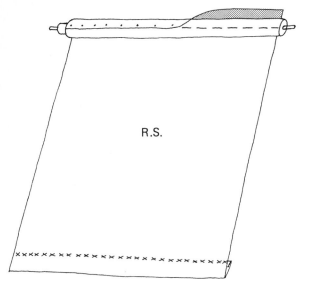

Fig. 174 **Positioning the blind to the roller**

make a casing for the wooden lath. Machine along the hem using a zigzag stitch (fig. 173). If straight stitching has to be used, take care to keep a straight

line when machining, and mark a guide line first.

(d) Position the blind to the roller as in fig 174, making sure that the right side is uppermost, that the sprung end of the roller is at the left hand side of the fabric, and that the fabric hangs close to the window. Place the fabric to the guide line provided on the roller and tack down every 3.8 cm (1½ in.) along the roller.

(e) Cut the wooden lath to the width of the blind and insert in the casing at the bottom of the blind. Knot one end of the pull cord and thread through the acorn fitting. Screw the fitment to the wrong side of the blind (fig. 175).

(f) The bottom edge of the blind can be decorated with fringing, or a piece of blind fabric can be cut to the shape chosen, suitably trimmed and fixed to the back of the casing with adhesive (fig. 176).

Fig. 175 **Acorn fitting screwed into position**

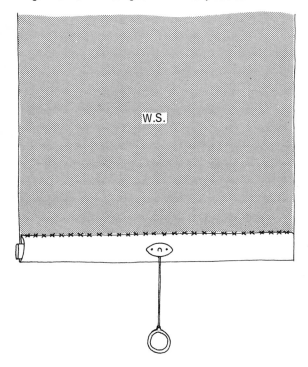

Fig. 176 **Applying a decorative edge to the wrong side of the roller blind**

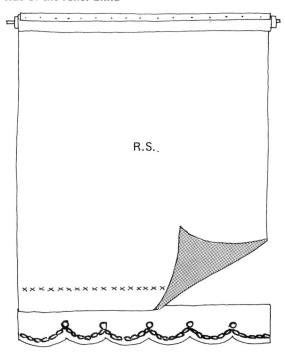

9 · Dressing Table Draperies

Dressing tables can be draped and decorated in many attractive styles. Traditional kidney-shaped whitewood tables with drawers at each side, and a curtain rail fixed below the table top, are probably the most popular choice. However, any small table or chest of drawers, or even a simple shelf, can be dressed to suit the decor of a bedroom. The top of the table is covered with fabric and should be protected by a piece of plate glass. A curtain rail is fixed underneath the table top, from which hang a pair of lined or unlined curtains. The curtains meet at the centre front and the headings are covered by a small pelmet which is fixed to the dressing table top.

Suitable fabrics range from furnishing cottons to voile and organdie, depending on the style chosen. Drapes for dressing tables can often be matched successfully to curtains or bedspreads, but can look equally as effective if made in a fabric of a different texture.

MAKING THE CURTAINS

These can be lined or unlined depending on the fabric chosen. For flimsy voiles and organdies allow two to three times the width of the curtain track, or enough fulness to conceal the woodwork underneath. For furnishing cottons and fabrics with more body, one and a half to twice the width of the track is sufficient. The curtains should be made to finish 1.3 cm (½ in.) from the floor and should meet with an overlap at the centre front. They can then be drawn back for easy access to drawers and storage space. As the heading of the curtains is covered by a pelmet, a simple gathered type of heading should be applied. To make the curtains, follow the instructions on pages 59 and 60.

COVERING THE DRESSING TABLE TOP

(a) Cut a paper pattern of the top of the table. From this pattern cut one piece of Vilene or bonded interfacing.

(b) Cut out the fabric and the lining, using the paper pattern, cutting both 2.5 cm (1 in.) larger all round to allow for turnings. Centralize any designs on the cover fabric if necessary.

Fig. 177 **Dressing table fabric herringbone stitched into position**

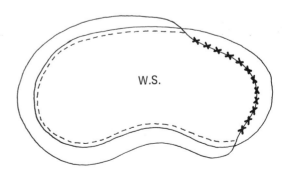

93

(c) Place the interfacing to the wrong side of the cover fabric and tack. Turn over the 2.5 cm (1 in.) seam allowance to the wrong side and herringbone into position (fig. 177).

(d) Apply the lining to the wrong side of the top cover turning in 2.5 cm (1 in.) all round and slipstitch into position (fig. 178).

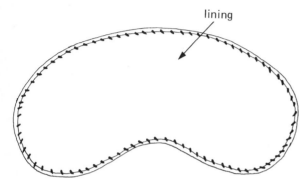

Fig. 178 **Lining applied to wrong side of dressing table cover**

MAKING THE PELMET

For the preparation and working of the pelmet, see page 85. Pelmet buckram or heavy Vilene can also be used as a foundation, but the buckram is not washable. To avoid powder and dust collecting in the pockets at the top edge of the pelmet, the following method of fixing should be used. Do not apply tape to the top edge of the pelmet but pin it in position to the cover of the dressing table top, starting at the centre front, then slipstitch neatly in place.

When designing a pelmet for a dressing table do not make the pelmet too deep or it will interfere with the smooth working of the drawers. Suit the design of the pelmet to the fabric, using any pattern to advantage (fig. 179). If plain fabric is used the pelmet can be decorated with embroidery, patchwork or quilting to give an individual finish.

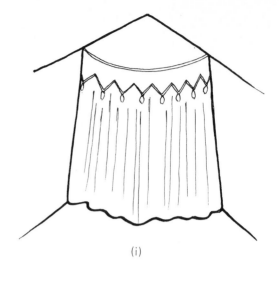

(i)

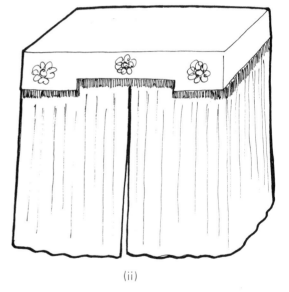

(ii)

Fig. 179 **Ideas for dressing table draperies: (i) tassels decorate the pelmet; (ii) patchwork motifs decorate the pelmet; (iii) a ruched edge used to trim the pelmet; (iv) pelmet trimmed with piping cord; (v) drapes used round a vanitory unit**

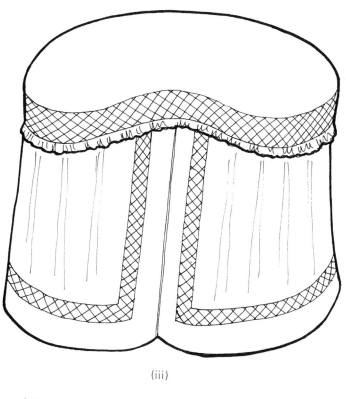

(iii)

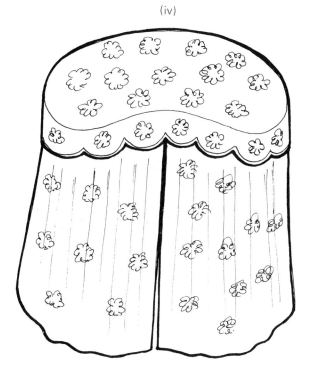

(iv)

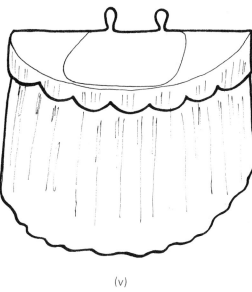

(v)

95

10-Loose Covers

A loose cover is a cover that can be easily removed from the chair for laundering or dry cleaning. It should be tailored to fit the chair, and when well-made, should have the appearance of a fitted upholstered chair. The cover should not be loose and baggy, as the name perhaps implies.

A loose cover protects the upholstery of the chair from dirt and dust. When recovering an old chair, make sure that the chair is cleaned thoroughly before the cover is made, otherwise the dirt will work through the fibres of the fabric and damage it. Check also that the structure of the chair is sound.

Loose covers can be used for most chairs and settees, and can give a new lease of life to a divan, small stool, pouffe or ottoman. Sufficient time must be allowed to plan and cut a cover accurately, especially when using large quantities of expensive fabric. First gain experience on small chairs and stools, then, when the techniques have been mastered, you can move on to tackle larger and more complicated covers.

CHOICE OF FABRIC

It is essential to choose the right type of fabric when making loose covers, otherwise time and effort will be wasted. The fabric must be sufficiently hard wearing to withstand regular drycleaning or laundering and so should be shrink and fade resistant. Choose fabric that is firm, smooth and closely woven. Loosely woven material is not suitable as it loses its shape quickly and does not wear well. Avoid using heavy tweeds and slubbed fabrics. These are more suitable for 'fitted' covers which are permanently upholstered to the chair. Linen union is perhaps the best choice of fabric for a loose cover, as it is hard wearing and crease resistant. It is available in a very wide range of patterns and a good range of plain colours. Other suitable fabrics include repp, cotton damask or other closely woven furnishing cottons. These will retain their shape and wear well if the cover is made correctly.

When choosing the fabric the decor of the room must be considered. Bear in mind that patterned fabrics do not show spots and dirt as quickly as plain or textured fabrics, and that any errors in construction are more apparent on plain fabrics.

A small pattern is easier to handle than a larger one, which needs to be centralized on several sections of the cover. This necessitates extra fabric for matching the patterns. Consider also the size of the chair when choosing patterned fabric, remembering that the effect of a large pattern might be lost on a small chair. A small all-over design might be more suitable, and would certainly be easier to work.

If possible use 80 cm (31 in.) wide fabric. This cuts more economically than 120 cm (48 in.) wide fabric. Unfortunately, not all

96

1   Bedspread, box cushions and curtains trimmed with matching
decorative braid (Courtesy Sanderson)

2 The traditional design of this pelmet complements the curtain fabric
(Courtesy Sanderson)

manufacturers make this width and it is not always obtainable.

Piping

All seams that define the outline of the chair should be piped. As well as strengthening the seams this gives a professional finish to the cover. The fabric used for piping can be of a contrasting colour, but it should be similar in weight and texture to that of the loose cover fabric. About ten metres (11 yards) of No. 2 or 3 piping cord is usually needed for an average sized chair cover.

MEASURING AND ESTIMATING

A rough estimate of the amount of fabric needed for a loose cover can be obtained by measuring five times the height of the back of the chair. However, before buying the fabric it is necessary to obtain a more accurate estimate, and the following measurements should be taken with a tape measure, to find the total amount of fabric needed. Figure 180 gives the names of each section.

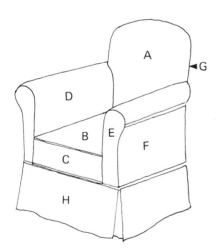

Fig. 180 **Terminology for the sections of a loose cover: (A) inside back; (B) seat; (C) front border; (D) inside arm; (E) front panel; (F) outside arm; (G) outside back; (H) frill**

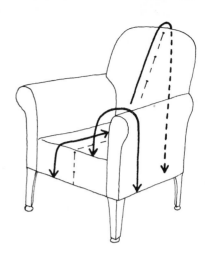

Fig. 181 **Taking the measurements of a chair with a 'fixed' edge**

(i)   The bottom of the outside back to the top of the back, down the inside back to the seat, plus 20.5 cm (8 in.) for tuck-away and turnings (fig. 181).

(ii) The back of the seat to the front of the seat down to the bottom of the front border, plus 20.5 cm (8 in.) for tuck-away and turnings (fig. 181).

(iii) The bottom of the outside arm, over the arm and down to the inside arm to the seat, plus 20.5 cm (8 in.) for tuck-away and turnings. Double this measurement to allow for the two arms (fig. 181).

The tuck-away is the fabric that is tucked in at the back and sides of the chair seat to hold the cover firmly in position and 15-20.5 cm (6-8 in.) is normally allowed for this. It is important to make this allowance otherwise the cover will slip out of place with the constant use of the chair.

Add these three measurements together to obtain the amount of 80 cm (31 in.) wide fabric needed. If using 120 cm (48 in.) wide fabric allow two thirds this amount.

To this total must be added ¾ - 1m (1 yd) for making the crossway strip to cover the piping cord. If a frill is being applied to the bottom of the cover an extra 1½-3 m (1½-3 yd) must be allowed, depending on the style of frill

97

chosen. Extra fabric must also be allowed for any loose cushions, allowing approximately 1 m (1 yd) for each cushion.

Each chair needs to be measured and planned individually, as each is different. However, the approximate amount of 80 cm (31 in.) wide fabric needed for making a cover for an average chair is 6½-7 m (7 yd). This assumes a plain or textured fabric (80 cm - 31 in. wide) and more is needed if a patterned fabric is used. An allowance of at least one pattern repeat must be made for centralizing and matching patterns.

Be generous when estimating fabric requirements and make sure that enough is obtained. It may not be possible to buy more of the same fabric when the cover needs to be renovated, and so it is advisable to have a little extra fabric left over to enable these repairs to be made.

Two sets of seat cushion covers and two sets of arm caps, made at the same time as the cover, considerably extend the life of a loose cover. Allow 1 m (1 yd) of 80 cm (31 in.) fabric for each arm cap.

MAKING THE CHAIR COVER

Cutting out the cover

A loose cover should always be cut on the chair. Never use a paper pattern (except for wings and small panels) and do not be tempted to unpick an old cover and use it as a pattern. It will almost certainly have stretched or shrunk and have lost its original shape.

(a) Make sure the chair is clean and the structure sound.

(b) The fabric is fitted on one half of the chair only using double fabric, so that when cut out both sides are identical. Find the centre of the chair by measuring with a tape measure and mark down the centre of the outside back, inside back and along the centre of the seat and down the front border. Use pins or tailor's chalk.

(c) Make small identification labels to attach to each section as it is cut out.

(d) When cutting out each section make sure that the straight of the grain runs to the floor. A chair is not always upright and may be slightly tilted, so this should be checked carefully.

(e) With right sides outside, so that any pattern can be easily seen, fold the fabric in half lengthwise. Place the fold to the centre line on the inside back of the chair (fig. 182). Sufficient fabric

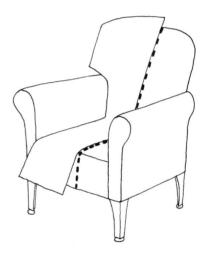

Fig. 182 **Laying fabric on the chair with fold to marked guide line**

must project beyond the top of the chair to allow for 5 cm (2 in.) turnings. If the fabric is patterned, make sure any motif is centralized. Allow 10-20.5 cm (6-8 in.) for tuck-away at the lower edge of the inside back section. Cut off fabric. Pin on label to identify the section.

(f) Place the folded fabric onto the seat in the same way, allowing 10-20.5 cm (6-8 in.) for tuck-away at the back and 5 cm (2 in.) for turnings at the front. Cut out and pin on label to identify.

(g) Cut out the front border in the same way allowing 5 cm (2 in.) for turnings if a frill is being applied to the bottom of the chair cover. Approximately 18 cm (7 in.) should be allowed if the cover is to tie underneath the chair without a frill. Pin on label to identify.

(h) The outside back is cut in the same way allowing 5 cm (2 in.) at the lower edge if a frill is being made and 18 cm (7 in.) if it is to tie underneath the chair. Pin on label to identify.

(i) With the right sides outside, join the outside back to the inside back at the top edge of the chair, using a continuous line of pins. Pin the lower edge of the inside back to the seat and the front of the seat to the front border.

(j) Cut the inside and outside arms separately, using a single piece of fabric and centralizing any pattern. 5 cm (2 in.) turnings must be allowed at the front to join with the front panel and at the back to join with the inside back. 5 cm (2 in.) turnings must also be allowed at the top of the inside and outside arms. Pin on labels to identify.

(k) The front panels must also be cut separately using single fabric and, if patterned material is being used, care must be taken to place a suitable motif on each front panel so that they both match.

(l) When all these pieces have been cut out, unpin all the sections and check that identifying labels are attached to each piece.

Fitting the cover

(a) Position all the sections and pin together on the chair with the right sides inside. Follow the lines of the chair when pinning, so that the seams that are to be piped define this line when the cover is completed (fig. 183).

(b) When there is a 'fixed' edge to a chair, that is one with an unsprung edge (fig. 181), the tuck-away seams must be carefully tapered from nothing at the

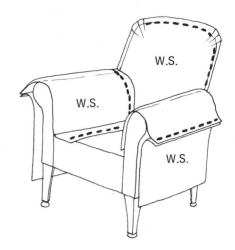

Fig. 183 **Pinning sections together on a chair with right sides inside**

front border to 15-20 cm (6-8 in.) at the back of the seat. If there is an 'independent' edge to a chair, one which has a sprung edge (fig. 184), the loose cover must fit down into this 'V' where the front border joins up with the front panel; this allows the spring to work independently. If this is not done the fabric will tear after a short time due to the constant movement of the springs.

Fig. 184 **'Independent' edge showing V where front border joins with front panel, to enable the springs to work independently**

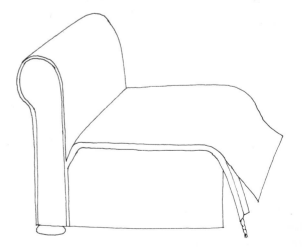

(c) Make darts if necessary, to take in any excess fullness on the inside back. This will depend on the shape of the chair.

(d) When the cover is satisfactorily pinned, trim off any surplus fabric to leave 2.5 cm (1 in.) turnings. Snip curves where necessary.

(e) Check pin lines again and adjust until a perfect fit is obtained. Make sure that each pin is firmly placed in the fabric.

(f) Remove the cover and tack the tuck-away seams and any darts that have been made.

Applying the piping

Prepare about 10m (10 yd) of piping cord and cover with crossway strip (see page 27). The piping cord should be prepared by pre-shrinking it by boiling for five minutes and drying thoroughly before use.

Always apply the piping to the section of the loose cover that takes the shape of the chair, i.e. the outside back, the outside arms, the front border and the front panels, clipping crossway round curves. These sections fit well and do not need darts. The other sections that are applied to them are the ones that sometimes need to be eased or darted to make them fit.

(a) Remove a few pins at a time and apply the piping cord and crossway along the top edge of the outside arms. Pin and tack, using small tacking stitches and matching thread. If worked in matching thread these tacking stitches do not need to be removed when the cover is finished. Re-pin carefully and tack the side seam together.

(b) Remove the pins carefully and apply the piping and crossway to the top edge of the front border in the same way. Re-pin and tack.

(c) Apply piping and crossway round the front panels in the same way except at the lower edges where they meet the front border. Re-pin and tack. It is sometimes easier to apply the piping to

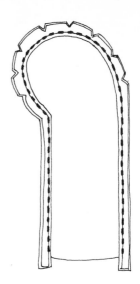

Fig. 185 **Piping applied to front panel**

the front panels before fitting these sections on to the chair (fig. 185).

(d) Most chair covers need an opening at the back to enable the cover to be removed easily. Mark the position for this. Remove pins and apply piping and crossway to the outside back as far as the top of the opening. At this point cross over the piping and apply it to the outside arm so that the opening is made as inconspicuous as possible when the cover is finished.

(e) Tack any remaining seams before fitting the cover on to the chair, wrong sides outside. Make any final adjustments that may be necessary, and then remove the cover from the chair.

Machining the cover

(a) Machine any darts on the inside back.

(b) Machine the tuck-away seams, starting at the front border on one side, and finishing at the front border on the other side.

(c) Machine stitch the piped seams in the following order: outside arms; front border; front panels; outside back as far as the opening. When machining a piped seam use a zipper foot if possible. This ensures that the stitching is as close as possible to the piping cord. If a zipper foot is not available let the machine foot rest on the piping cord when working and the stitching should then be close to the cord. Where two piped seams meet, pull out the piping cord from one seam and cut off 2.5 cm (1 in.). This makes the seam less bulky.

(d) For extra strength make another row of machine stitching 0.6 cm (¼ in.) away from the first on all seams.

(e) Trim all seams 1.3 cm (½ in.), and neaten the edges.

Fig. 186 **Chair with a gathered frill, showing position of piping**

FRILLS

A frill is often attached to the bottom of the chair cover and this can be made in different styles to suit the individual chair and the fabric being used. As well as hiding unsightly legs it makes an attractive finish to the chair (fig. 186).

Measuring and preparing the frill

(a) Try the cover on the chair and mark the base line, i.e. the position for the piping and the frill. This line should be marked using tailor's chalk or a line of pins. Measure with a ruler or meter stick the height from the floor where the piping cord will be applied. Care must be taken to see that the base line is marked the same distance from the floor all round. Chairs are often lower at the back than at the front and this point must be checked carefully (fig. 187).

The frill can vary in depth from 15 to 20 cm (6 to 8 in.) according to the size and type of chair, and should finish 1.3 cm (½ in.) from the floor. Allow 1.3 cm (½ in.) for turnings at the top of the frill and 3.8 cm (1½ in.) for the bottom hem. The frill can be made in the following styles.

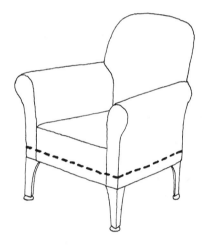

Fig. 187 **Guide line marked for frill**

Gathered frill This is a very attractive finish for a small chair where the fabric drapes well and is suitable for gathering. Allow one and a half times the measurement round the base line.

Box-pleated frill This gives a more tailored finish but uses more fabric. Allow three times the measurement round the base line for this type of frill.

101

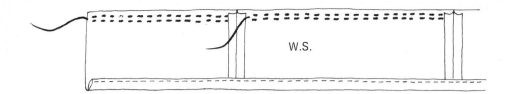

W.S.

Fig. 188 **Making a frill**

Inverted corner pleats   This is a tailored finish which uses much less fabric than a box-pleated frill. Measure the base line and allow 40 cm (16 in.) extra for each corner pleat, plus turning allowance.

(b)   The frill is cut out and prepared before applying it to the cover.

(c)   Cut strips of fabric across the width of the fabric (i.e. from selvedge to selvedge) the required depth of the frill, plus turnings. The length of the strip is of course determined by the style of the frill. Make sure any patterns are matched and that the bottom of the pattern comes at the hem.

(d)   Tack and machine the strips together using 1.3 cm (½ in.) turnings. Press the seams open. Make a 1.3 cm (½ in.) double machined hem along the lower edge (fig. 188).

(e)   Pin and tack the piping and crossway along the base guide line.

Applying the frill to the cover
Gathered frill

(a)   Divide and mark the strip into four and run two rows of gathering stitches 1.3 cm (½ in.) from the top edge along each section, using a separate thread for each section (fig. 188).

(b)   Divide the base line of the loose cover into four equal sections. Pin the frill to the cover, matching sections. Start pinning at the back opening at the outside arm and continue round the cover finishing at the outside back.

(c)   Draw up the gathering threads to fit into each section on the cover. Adjust gathers and tack into position.

(d)   Machine the frill to the cover, using a zipper foot and making two rows of stitching 0.6 cm (¼ in.) apart. Neaten edges.

Box-pleated frill

(a)   Prepare the strips of fabric.

(b)   Pleats can be formed in several ways, but equidistant box pleats are the most usual choice. To make 5 cm (2 in.) equidistant pleats, mark out as for a box-pleated heading, page 74. The size of the pleats and spaces can, of course, be varied to suit individual requirements. Care must be taken when planning the pleating to make sure that a pleat is positioned at each corner of the front of the cover.

(c)   Pin the frill to the cover, starting at the back opening. Begin with a space and continue pinning, arranging a pleat at each corner of the front of the cover. If possible, both ends of the front border should start with half a space (fig. 190). Alternatively a pleat must be placed at each corner as in fig. 191. A little adjustment to the pleat may be necessary to achieve this arrangement, but it is important to make sure that the pleating on the front border is correct, as it is in a very prominent position.

Frill with inverted corner pleats

(a)   Prepare the strips of fabric.

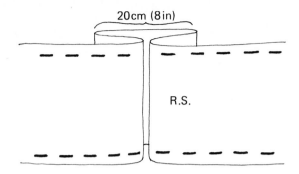

Fig. 189 **Making an inverted pleat for a corner**

20cm (8in)

R.S.

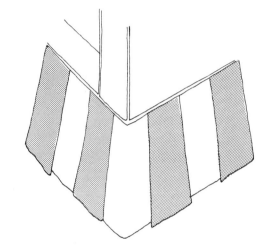

Fig. 190 **Arranging the pleats at a corner**

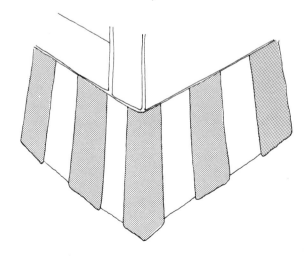

Fig. 191 **Alternative arrangement of pleats**

(b) Make an inverted 20 cm (8 in.) pleat (a box pleat in reverse) for each corner of the cover and tack firmly into position (fig. 189).

(c) Pin the frill to the cover, matching corner pleats to the corners of the cover. At the back opening arrange half an inverted pleat at each side of the opening.

(d) Tack and machine into position using a zipper foot and two rows of machine stitching. Neaten edges.

TIE-UNDER FINISH

When a cover is finished without a frill it is necessary to tie it underneath the chair in order to make it stay in position. When cutting out the cover an allowance of 18 cm (7 in.) will have been made on the outside back, outside arms and the front border for a tie-under finish (see page 98). This needs to be fitted round each chair leg, faced with bias binding, and a casing needs to be made for threading through the tape, which will then tie underneath the chair.

(a) Finish the opening at the back of the chair with a continuous wrap opening (page 49).

(b) With the cover on the chair, mark the position of the feet with tailor's chalk, allowing 1.3 cm (½ in.) for turnings. Slash up at each leg carefully fitting the fabric round the leg and cutting away surplus fabric (figs 192 and 193).

(c) Remove the cover from the chair, and face the cut-away edges with bias binding or crossway strip of matching fabric.

(d) Make a 1.3 cm (½ in.) hem at the bottom edge of the four flaps (fig. 194) to form a casing for the tape.

(e) Thread a piece of strong tape through the four casings.

(f) Place the cover in position on the chair and tie the tapes firmly underneath the chair (fig. 195).

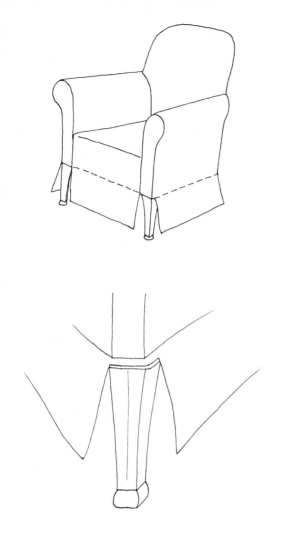

Figs. 192 and 193 **Slashing fabric at corner to fit round leg**

OPENINGS FOR LOOSE COVERS

Finish openings on loose covers with a continuous wrap using hooks and bars or Velcro to give added strength. A zip can be used, but choose one that is strong enough to take considerable strain. Except in the case of a tie-under finish, the opening should be worked when the frill has been applied.

SETTEES, WING CHAIRS AND STOOLS

Settees
The same basic principles apply when making other types of loose covers. A settee cover is treated in exactly the same way as a chair cover, except that additional width is required to cover the two or three seats. Fabric should be carefully matched across the inside back of the settee, but if necessary the pieces can be piped to divide the sections on the inside back (fig. 196).

Wing chairs
When making a chair cover for a wing chair the same techniques apply, but separate pieces should be cut for the front and back wing sections to make the cover sit well. A paper pattern can be made, if necessary, before cutting out the fabric. Allow 2.5 cm (1 in.) for turnings, and an allowance for a tuck-in if there is one. The inside of the wing may require darts, and these should be tacked and tried onto the chair before machining (fig. 197).

Stools
When making covers for stools and boxes, follow the same basic rules and principles for making loose covers for chairs. The fabric for the top of the box or stool is cut to the required size, plus 1.3 cm (½ in.) turnings all round. If possible, always make a border, as this holds the cover in position. Cut four separate pieces for the borders and allow 1.3 cm (½ in.) turnings all round (fig. 198). Do not make the borders deeper than the depth of the frill, or the stool will not look well proportioned.

Always apply the piping to the top sections of stools and boxes and not to the borders. When applying piping to a circular top section remember to snip the crossway strip when applying it, so that it moulds well to the curved edge.

The frill is made in the same way as for a chair cover and, if pleated, care must be

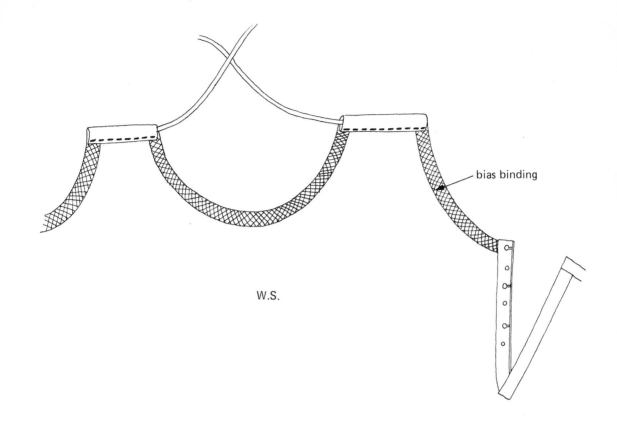

bias binding

W.S.

Fig. 194 Tie-under finish; outside arm section showing hem at lower edge and continuous wrap opening

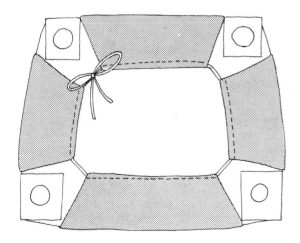

Fig. 195 Tapes tied in position underneath chair

Fig. 196 Sections piped on settee cover

taken to position the pleats correctly at the corners. In the case of a round stool, the final join should make a complete space and pleat (fig. 199).

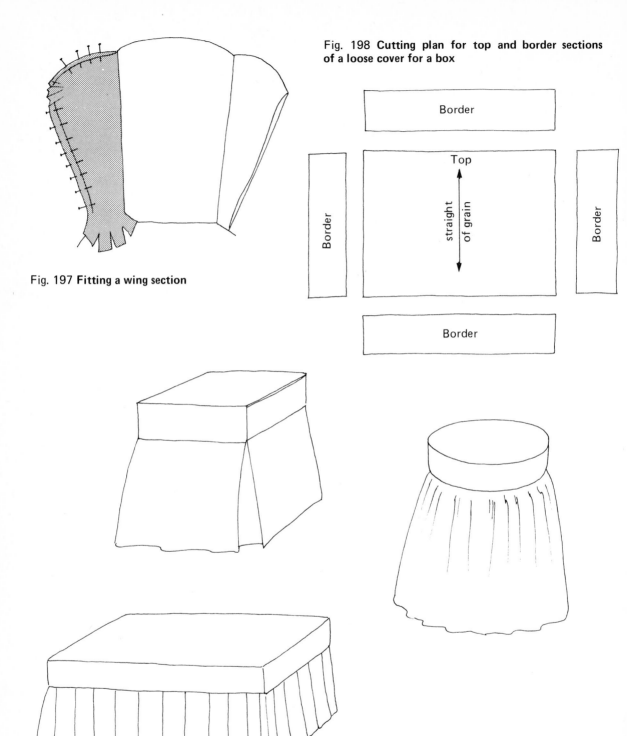

Fig. 197 **Fitting a wing section**

Fig. 198 **Cutting plan for top and border sections of a loose cover for a box**

Border

Border

Top

straight
of grain

Border

Border

Fig. 199 **Styles for stools or boxes**

11 · Bedspreads and Valances

A bedspread is often the main focal point in a bedroom. In small, modern homes where space is limited, the bed provides the largest expanse of colour or texture; it may be the only piece of furniture in the room apart from fitted cupboards. Therefore, the choice of bed coverings, whether they are bedspreads or duvet covers, is very important, as it is these that provide the most impact.

CHOICE OF FABRIC

Simple throw-over bedspreads are easy to make and their success or otherwise lies in the choice of fabric. Care should be taken to choose styles for bedspreads that suit the fabric. For example, if a gathered frill is planned, the fabric must have good draping qualities. For pleating, a firmer fabric which presses easily is required. Choose crease-resistant fabrics that are reasonably hard wearing, and that launder or dry clean easily. It is particularly important to choose easy-care fabrics for children's bedrooms.

Bedspreads and valances can match curtains and wallpaper if the fabric is suitable, but beware of having too much pattern in a small room — this can have an overpowering effect. Instead, mix plain and patterned fabrics together to give a more interesting overall scheme.

When choosing a printed patterned fabric remember to check that the pattern is printed correctly on the grain of the fabric, otherwise it will be difficult to match the patterns and make up successfully. Remember, also, that small patterns are easier to handle and are often more suitable than very large ones. Large patterns may be effective in expansive hotel bedrooms, but may prove rather disappointing when used in small modern rooms. Furnishing cottons, dupions, glazed cottons, cotton lace, sheeting and many of the man-made fabrics, are all suitable for making attractive bedcovers and valances.

Fig. 200 **Taking the measurements of the bed: (A) length; (B) width; (C) height**

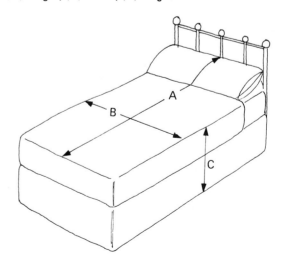

TAKING THE MEASUREMENTS

All measurements for bedspreads should be taken when the bed is made up with the usual amount of bedclothes and pillows. The following measurements are those usually needed to estimate the amount of fabric required (fig. 200): the top of the bed to the foot of the bed; the width of the bed; the height of the bed from the floor to the top of the bed.

Each bed should be measured individually. For a fitted bedspread the height of the pillow must also be measured. It is usual to line all bedspreads, except throw-over ones made from very firm fabrics. When choosing a lining fabric make sure it has the same washing or dry cleaning qualities as those of the bedspread fabric. Allow 2.5 cm (1 in.) turnings on all sections when making up bedspreads.

THROW-OVER BEDSPREADS

Straight throw-over bedspread

This style of bedspread is the easiest to make and usually 5.75 m (6 yards) of 120 cm (48 in.) wide fabric is sufficient to make a bedspread in a plain fabric for a standard-length bed. This would be sufficient for a single bed or medium-sized double bed, but more would be required for a king-sized bed, and when matching large pattern repeats.

For a single bedspread, the width of the centre section may need to be reduced to the width of the bed before the side sections are applied. The side sections might need to be adjusted in size if a valance is being made, in order to allow the valance to show.

(a) Cut two widths of fabric, 2.75 m (3 yds) long, cut off all selvedges. Use one for the central section of the bedspread, then cut the other width in half lengthwise and join one to each side of the main section (fig. 201), so that the seams are down each side of the bed and

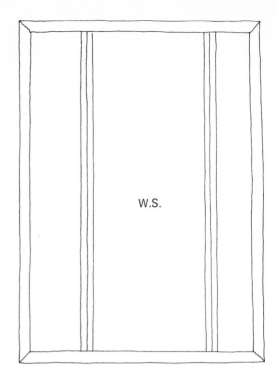

Fig. 201 Bedspread showing central section and two side sections seamed

not in the middle. These seams can be piped or covered with decorative braid. Any patterns must be carefully matched.

(b) With right sides together, make a flat seam and press it open. If a lining is not being used, make a run and fell seam, finishing it by hand.

(c) Turn in both sides and the bottom edge of the bedspread 1.3 cm (½ in.). Mitre each corner and make a 3.8 cm (1½ in.) hem. Slipstitch by hand (figs. 202 and 203).

(d) The corners at the foot of the bed can be rounded as in fig. 204, using a large plate to obtain the curve shape. Cut one side first and then fold over to match the other side to it exactly.

(e) To make the lining for the bedspread cut out and seam the lining in the same way as the cover.

(f) With wrong sides together apply the

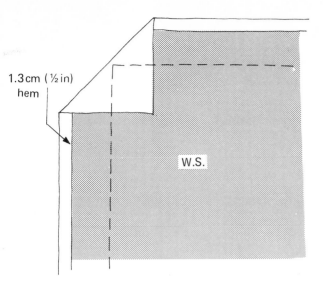

1.3cm (½ in) hem

W.S.

Fig. 202 **Corner mitre showing positions for folds**

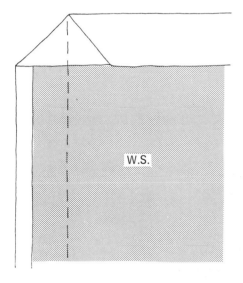

W.S.

Fig. 203 **Corner mitre showing first fold and position for second fold**

lining to the cover, matching seams. Lockstitch together along the seam.

(g) Turn in the lining and tack to the bedspread 2.5 cm (1 in.) from the edge all round. Slipstitch into position.

(h) For a bed with a footboard, the side

sections should be cut as in fig. 205 to allow for the footboard.

Throw-over bedspreads can be decorated with braid, fringing or appliqué. They are also most attractive when worked in English quilting or patchwork.

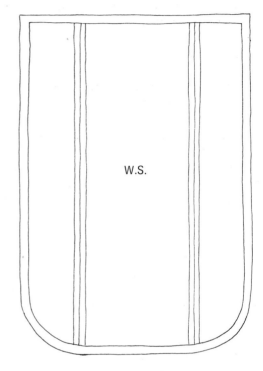

W.S.

Fig. 204 **Bedspread with curved ends**

Lace throw-over bedspread

White cotton lace can be used to make a throw-over bedspread. This is obtainable by the metre (yard) in widths suitable for both single and double beds, so that seams are unnecessary.

Cut the bedspread to the length and width required and make a 2.5 cm (1 in.) double hem at the top edge. The sides and bottom edges of the bedspread look attractive if the lace is scalloped to show off the pattern to advantage. These edges can then be bound with crossway strip or bias binding, or trimmed with a suitable fabric.

109

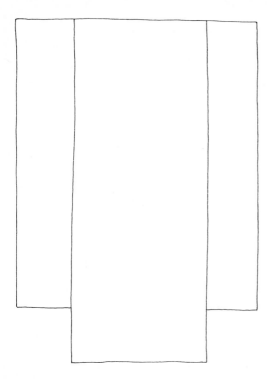

Fig. 205 **Cutting a bedspread to allow for a foot-board**

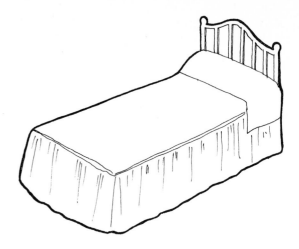

Fig. 206 **Bedspread with pillow flap in position**

This type of bedspread looks most effective when used over coloured blankets, or made with a coloured lining. A valance over the base of the bed completes the style.

BEDSPREAD WITH A PILLOW FLAP

When making a flap to fold over the pillows, extra fabric must be allowed on the platform length. This is usually about 75 cm (30 in.), but the distance over the pillows should be measured carefully, and added to that of the required length for the platform.

The pillow flap must be made wide enough to allow it to overhang the ends of the pillows and at least 30.5 cm - 35.5 cm (12-14 in.) of fabric may need to be added at each side of the flap. The pillow flap should be finished to match the bedspread frill and should be lined (figs. 206 and 207).

Cut off the pillow flap at the top of the platform, place the right side of the platform to the wrong side of the pillow flap (fig. 208). Tack and machine. This reverses the fabric so that when the pillows are placed in position on the platform the pillow flap comes over the top of the pillows with the right side outside.

FITTED BEDSPREAD WITH A PILLOW GUSSET

A fitted bedspread, like a loose cover, must fit well, and the same basic principles and techniques should be applied when making up. Allow 2.5 cm (1 in.) turnings when cutting out.

A fitted bedspread for a divan has a frill at the two sides and one at the bottom edge (figs. 209 and 210). The platform is the piece of fabric that covers the top of the bed and tucks over and behind the pillow. When cutting out the platform for a fitted bedspread, allow approximately 25.5 - 30.5 cm (10-12 in) extra on the length of the bed to allow for the height of the pillows and for the tuck-away at the back of the pillows.

110

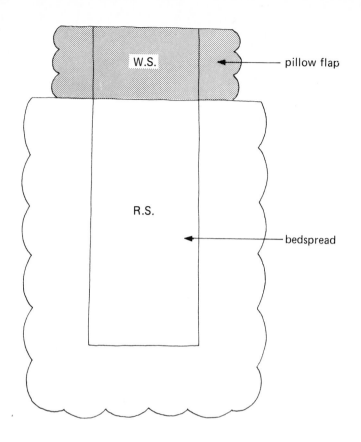

pillow flap

W.S.

R.S.

bedspread

▲

Fig. 207 Pillow flap reversed and stitched into position at the top of the platform section

Fig. 208 Wrong side of pillow flap stitched to right ➤ side of bedspread

Fig. 209 Fitted bedspread with pillow gusset

▼

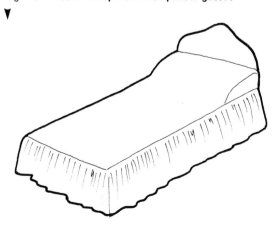

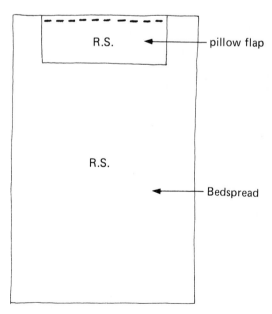

R.S.

pillow flap

R.S.

Bedspread

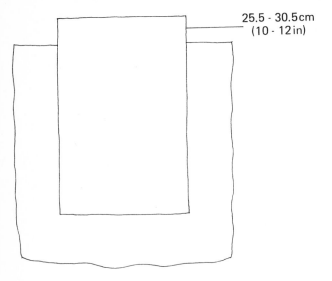

Fig. 210 **Fitted bedspread with pillow gusset showing 25.5 cm - 30.5 cm (10-12 in.) allowance for tucking in at the back of the pillows**

In order to make the bedspread fit well an extra piece of fabric is inserted at the head of the bed to allow for the bedspread to rise over the pillows without lifting it off the ground. This insertion is called a pillow gusset and its size should be determined by the size and number of pillows used. For a standard pillow that measures 50 x 75 cm (19 x 29 in.) the pillow gusset should be made to finish 50-51 cm (20 in.) long. Its height should be 12.5 cm (5 in.) to allow for one pillow or 25.5 cm (10 in.) to allow for two pillows (fig. 211).

(a) Cut out the platform and the lining to the required length and add any additional widths as described on page 108. Join with a flat seam and press open.

(b) Make a paper pattern of the gusset to fit the individual pillow requirements. From this cut out two pillow gussets for the bedspread, taking care to position the paper pattern correctly on the fabric so that any pattern is the same at each side of the bedspread. Cut out one for the left side and one for the right hand side.

(c) Also from the pattern cut out two pieces of lining and two pieces of interlining (Vilene or non-woven interfacing). Interlining helps the gusset to hold its shape well, particularly if the fabric is soft.

(d) Tack or iron the interlining onto the wrong side of the pillow gusset.

(e) Pin and tack the piping along the top and back edges of the gusset (fig. 212) clipping curves. Machine.

Fig. 212 **Piping tacked to right side of pillow gusset**

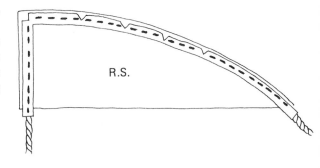

R.S.

Fig. 211 **Cutting the gusset**

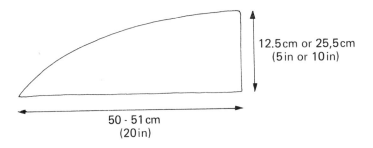

12.5 cm or 25,5 cm
(5 in or 10 in)

50 - 51 cm
(20 in)

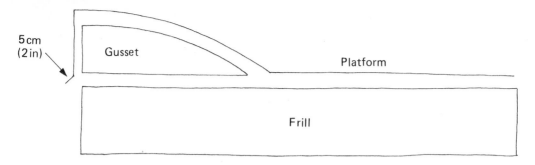

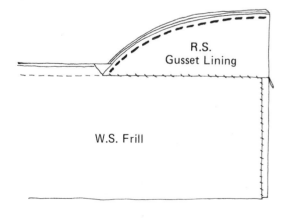

Fig. 213 Position of sections showing 5 cm (2 in.) allowance for hem at the top edge of the platform

(f) Pin the pillow gusset to the platform positioning the gusset so that there is a 5 cm (2 in.) allowance for a hem at the top edge of the platform (fig. 213). Machine.

(g) Pin and tack the piping to the platform, starting at the back of one pillow gusset and continue round to the back of the other. Machine.

Making the frill

(a) Cut out and prepare the frill as for a loose cover (page 101). Always cut the frill across the fabric, i.e. with the selvedge running down.

(b) Join the frill pieces together with flat seams and press open. On the two short

Fig. 214 Double hem, 1.3 cm (½ in.), stitched on frill; curved edge of gusset lining tacked to matching seam of platform section

ends of the frill, which will be positioned at the head of the bed, make 1.3 cm (½ in.) double hems and stitch by hand (fig. 214).

(c) Measure and mark the platform into eight equal sections, and mark and measure the frill in the same way.

(d) If a gathered frill is being made, two rows of running stitches should be made along each section and must be drawn up to fit each section on the platform.

(e) With right sides together, pin the platform sections to the frill matching marks and adjusting the gathers to fit. Tack and machine into position.

(f) If pleats are being used for the frill, care must be taken to position the corner pleats correctly (figs. 190 and 191).

Lining the bedspread

(a) With right sides together join the short back edge of the pillow gusset lining to the platform lining, leaving 5 cm (2 in.) extending for turnings at the top edge of the platform (fig. 215).

(b) Lay the platform lining to the wrong side of the platform of the bedspread, matching seams. Fold back the lining to each seam and lockstitch into position on the seams (fig. 216). Tack the lining into position approximately 10 cm (4 in.) from the piped edge.

(c) Pin the long straight side of the pillow gusset lining to the frill, turning in 1.3 cm (½ in.) and enclosing the raw edges. Tack and hem by hand.

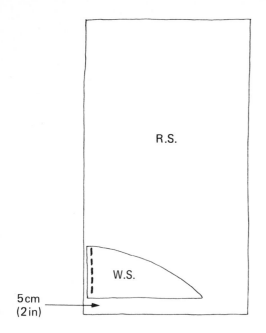

Fig. 215 **Pillow gusset lining tacked to platform lining leaving a 5 cm (2 in.) turning allowance**

(d) Pin and tack the curved edge of the pillow gusset lining to the matching seam of the bedspread (fig. 214). Machine into position.

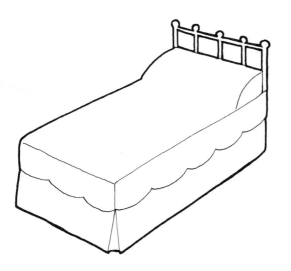

Fig. 216 **Fitted bedspread with scalloped frill and valance**

(e) Turn under the platform lining round the two sides and bottom and enclose all the raw edges. Tack. Hem into position by hand.

FITTED BEDSPREAD WITH A SCALLOPED FRILL

A scalloped frill makes an attractive finish for a fitted bedspread and can be used with a matching or contrasting valance (fig. 216).

(a) Prepare the platform, piping and pillow gusset of the bedspread as on page 110.
(b) Measure the depth and length required for the frill, making sure that the scalloped edge finishes 5-7.5 cm (2-3 in.) below the valance (fig. 217). Make a paper pattern for one side section of the bed and the end section.

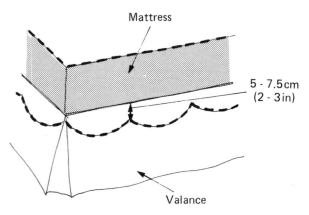

Fig. 217 **Lower edge of bedspread frill positioned 5 - 7.5 cm (2 - 3 in.) below the top of the valance**

(c) Plan the scallops to fit into the length and width of the frill. Mark and cut out the paper pattern.
(d) Cut two pieces of fabric for the side sections and one for the end section, using the paper pattern, and allowing 1.3 cm (½ in.) turnings. Cut out lining and interling to match.

114

(e) Join the side section to the end section on both lining and fabric, taking 1.3 cm (½ in.) turnings.

(f) Iron or tack the interlining onto the wrong side of the frill fabric on all sections.

(g) With right sides facing, pin and tack the lining to the scalloped edge, taking 1.3 cm (½ in.) turnings (fig. 218). Tack up to the top of each scallop at the end of the two side sections. Machine along the tacking line. Trim seams to 0.6 cm (¼ in.) and clip into curves. Turn to the right side and press.

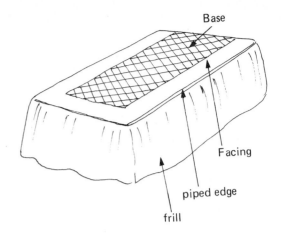

Fig. 219 **Valance covering base of bed**

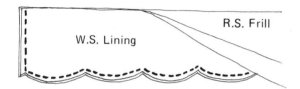

Fig. 218 **Lining tacked to scalloped edge**

(h) With right sides together, pin and tack the straight edge of the frill to the platform, matching corner seams.

(i) Finish lining on the platform as on page 113, enclosing the raw edges. Hem by hand.

MAKING A VALANCE

A valance is slipped over the base of the bed underneath the mattress and is often matched to fitted sheets and duvets. It is also attractive when used with throw-over and fitted bedspreads and can then be made in heavier matching or contrasting fabrics. When teaming a valance to a duvet cover or sheets, use polyester/cotton sheeting in matching or contrasting colours. This can be used for making the whole of the valance. If using dupion or other heavier fabric, economies can be made by using calico or sheeting for the valance base. The facings must, however, be made in the same fabric as the frill (fig. 219).

(a) Cut a piece of calico or polyester/cotton sheeting the size of the base plus 2.5 cm (1 in.) turnings. Pin and tack a 1.3 cm (½ in.) hem all round and machine.

(b) For a gathered frill allow one and a half times to twice the length of the frill round the base; for an inverted pleat at each of the bottom corners, allow the length of the finished frill plus 40.5 cm (16 in.) for each corner pleat.

(c) The depth of the frill can vary from 30.5 to 35.5 cm (12 to 14 in.) depending on the individual bed. When cutting out, allow 7.5 cm (3 in.) for turnings.

(d) For the three facings cut three strips of fabric 15 cm (6 in.) wide. Two must be the length of the bed base and one must be the width of the base. Allow 2.5 cm (1 in.) turnings on each strip when cutting out.

(e) Pin the facing strips to the calico base and mitre the two corners. Remove the facing from the calico and machine the mitred corners. leaving 1.3 cm (½ in.) unstitched at each end (figs 57-60).

(f) Join together the strips for the frill with 1.3 cm (½ in.) turnings. Press seams open.

115

Make a 1.3 cm (½ in.) double hem at the two short sides of the frill and a 2.5 cm (1 in.) double hem at the lower edge. These hems can be machined or worked by hand.

(g) Divide the calico base into six sections and mark with tailor's chalk (fig. 220).

(h) For a gathered frill, divide the length of the strip into six and make two rows of running stitches 1.3 cm (½ in.) from the top edge of each section. Draw up the gathering stitches and adjust so that they fit into each of the six sections. With the wrong sides together, pin and tack the frill to the calico base. For pleated corners, fold and arrange one inverted pleat at each bottom corner and tack into position with wrong sides facing.

(i) Prepare the crossway strip for the piped edge. Apply the piping and crossway strip to the calico, pinning and tacking over the gathered edge, taking particular care not to stretch it.

(j) Pin and tack the facing to the frill over the piping, matching the mitred corners to the corners of the valance. Keep the right side of the facing to the right side of the frill. Machine through all thicknesses along the two sides and the bottom edge of the valance.

(k) With the valance in position on the base, so that it is flat, turn in 1.3 cm (½ in.) along the raw edges of the facing and pin and tack to the calico base. Remove the valance from the base and machine, using a large zigzag stitch (fig. 221).

Fig. 221 **Valance facing stitched to base using a large zigzag stitch**

Fig. 220 **Base marked into six sections**

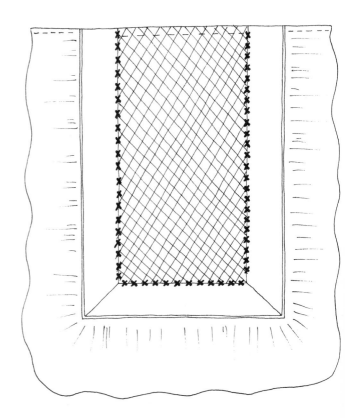

116

12-Patchwork

Patchwork is a most fascinating and rewarding craft and is a practical way of using up odd pieces of fabric left over when making other items of soft furnishing. Small or large patches of various shapes can be made and sewn together to decorate cushions, curtains, tie-backs, bedspreads table mats, pillow cases etc.

With a little imagination and a knowledge of the basic skills, interesting and original designs can be made using the range of patchwork templates available. These are used to cut out the paper shapes for each patch. A piece of fabric is then cut from the shape, allowing appropriate turnings, and is tacked to the paper shape. The patches are sewn together and the paper shapes removed when the work is finished.

Many specialist books have been written for those who wish to study this subject further (see the Bibliography at the end of this book) but for the beginner wishing to start the craft the following notes on the basic principles may serve as a useful introduction.

MATERIALS

Templates
It is essential that the templates are perfectly accurate and rigid so that the paper shapes can be cut from them. They should therefore be made from metal, Perspex or Plexiglass.

They are available in various shapes and sizes and are obtained from specialist firms or craft shops. The shapes used in patchwork are mostly geometric — hexagons, squares, and diamonds and variations on these. The hexagon shape is the one most often used by the beginner, but the same basic principles apply to all the geometric shapes (fig. 222).

Fabric
Patchwork originated as an economy craft and only oddments and left-over pieces of fabric were used. Now, however, fabric is often purchased especially for the craft. Choose fabrics that are of a similar weight and texture and which fold well. Avoid those which stretch or fray easily, as these will be difficult to handle. If an article needs regular laundering (e.g. place mats, pillow cases, etc.) make sure that all the fabrics used are easily washable and colour fast. If using transparent fabrics, a bonded interfacing can be used instead of card or stiff paper for cutting the shapes. This is left in the work and gives body to the finished article.

Card
Stiff paper or thin card is used for cutting out the shapes from the templates. Never use newspaper.

Scissors
Use an old pair of scissors for cutting out the paper shapes.

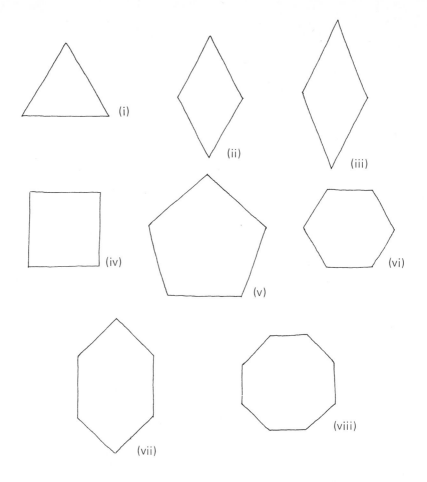

Thread
Use pure silk if using silk fabrics, synthetic thread for man-made fibres and cotton (No. 40-100) for cotton fabrics. Use black thread for sewing dark patches together and white for sewing light patches together.

METHOD

Cutting out the shapes
Draw round the template very carefully on the paper using a sharp pencil. Cut out the shapes as accurately as possible, so that the patches match up well.

Fig. 222 Geometric shapes used for patchwork: (i) triangle; (ii) diamond; (iii) long diamond; (iv) square; (v) pentagon; (vi) hexagon; (vii) long hexagon; (viii) octagon

Cutting out the fabric and tacking
Pin the paper shape to the wrong side of the fabric and cut out, allowing a seam allowance of 1 cm (3/8 in.) all round (fig. 223). Centre the pattern if necessary. This is best done by using a 'window' template. This is a template with a hole in the middle the size of the finished patch. The outside edge represents the seam allowance. The template can be laid onto the fabric and the design can be easily selected for each patch (fig. 224).

118

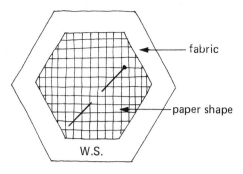

Fig. 223 **Pinning the paper shape to the wrong side of the fabric**

Use small stitches and as fine a needle as possible. Insert the needle at right angles (figs. 228 and 229), and start as near as possible to one corner. Work in the end of the thread as shown in fig. 229, and only pick up the fabric. Avoid sewing in the paper shape. Fasten off by working backwards for two or three stitches The stitches are not meant to be invisible on the right side of the work, but in order to achieve a neat appearance they should be worked as evenly and as straight as possible.

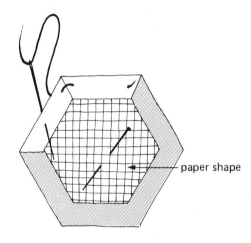

Fig. 225 **Tacking the fabric to the paper shape**

Fig. 224 **Using a window template to centralize a pattern**

Fold the seam allowance over the edge of the paper keeping the template parallel to the grain of the fabric. Tack as in figs 225 and 226 using a fine needle. If using glazed cotton, or fabrics that are marked easily by the needle, do not tack right through to the right side of the fabric, but cross tack as in fig. 227, or take the tacking stitches into the paper only.

Sewing the patches
Place the right sides of the two patches together and oversew them with a single thread.

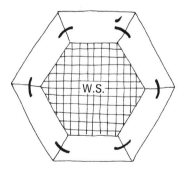

Fig. 226 **Fabric tacked to paper shape showing the position of stitching**

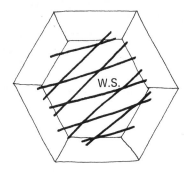

Fig. 227 **Fabric cross tacked to paper shape**

Finishing off

Patches are usually sewn up in small groups or motifs (figs. 230 and 231) and then joined together afterwards to form an overall design. When all patches have been sewn together, press gently with a warm iron on the wrong side. This helps the turnings to stay firmly in position. If the work needs pressing on the right side the paper shapes should be left in place to avoid the turnings making a mark.

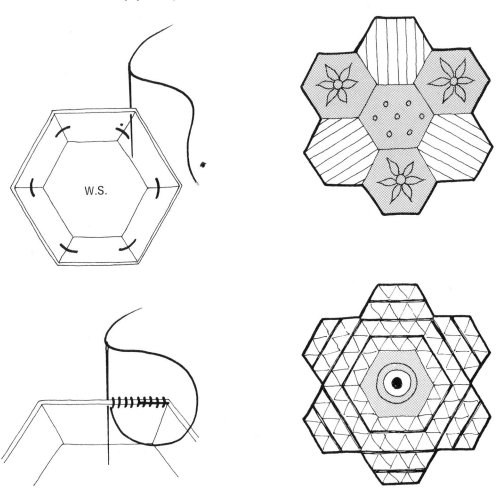

Figs. 228 and 229 **Sewing the patches together**   Fig. 230 **Designs using hexagons**

120

3 A simple loose cover used over a small table makes an attractive
dressing table to match the curtains and scalloped pelmet

4 Cotton lace bedspread with scalloped edge used over a gathered valance

5   Loose cover in linen union shown with a selection of cushion styles

6   The formal style of this pelmet is used to enhance the shape of this window

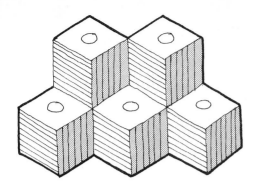

Fig. 231 **Design using diamonds**

Take out all the tackings and paper shapes and tack round the outer edges of the work to hold the turnings securely in position. The patchwork can then be made up as desired or applied to cushions, curtains, etc. using a small slipstitch. When working with large areas of patchwork, such as a quilt, the article should be lined and finished as below.

Considerable thought should be given to the design and grouping of the patches and this is best done by laying out the patches on a soft board or tray and experimenting with colour, pattern and texture until a pleasing effect is achieved.

PATCHWORK BEDSPREADS AND QUILTS

Patchwork should be mounted onto a firm foundation when making a bedspread or a quilt. A great deal of time and trouble is put into the making of a patchwork article of

this kind, and it is important to make sure that it is mounted correctly and that the edges are finished neatly. Use a firm cotton fabric to line a bedspread or quilt.

(a) Lay the patchwork onto a large flat surface and pin the lining to it wrong sides together. The lining should be cut to the exact size of the patchwork.

(b) For a single bedspread work three rows of lock stitch from the top of the quilt to the bottom (see fig. 106). For a double bedspread or quilt work five rows.

(c) Tack the lining in position 5 cm (2 in.) from each edge.

(d) Finish the edges in one of the following ways.
   (i) Bind the raw edges with crossway strip (page 36).
   (ii) Apply piping to the right side of the patchwork. Turn in the lining and slipstitch into position on the wrong side.
   (iii) Turn in the edge of the patchwork 1.3 cm (½ in.) and the lining 1.3 cm (½ in.) so that the turnings are inside the quilt. Work two rows of running stitches all round the quilt keeping the stitching close to the edges.

(e) Patchwork quilts and bedspreads can also be interlined using bump, domette or sheet Terylene wadding. This should be locked in position on the wrong side of the patchwork, and the lining should then be applied as explained above.

13· Quilting

Quilting is an attractive and reasonably quick method of decorating cushions, bedspreads lampshades and many other items for the home. These are three main types of quilting — English, Italian and Trapunto.

ENGLISH QUILTING

This is functional as well as decorative, and was probably first introduced into Europe in the eleventh and twelfth centuries. The craft flourished and developed in Wales and the northern counties of England and was first used as a means of holding three layers of fabric together to produce a suitable 'quilt' for a bed. Sheep's wool was gathered from the hedgerows and used for the padding between two pieces of fabric, and in the early days simple geometric designs were used to stitch the layers together. Later more attention was paid to the designs and a central motif was made using simple templates. These patterns have been handed down through the generations and are now known as traditional English quilting designs. There are many examples of exquisite traditional quilting to be seen in local and national museums and each one has a different story to tell. Particular signs and stitches were used in different localities, and it is possible for the expert to trace the place of origin and even the date of these beautiful examples of quilting.

Equipment
Fabrics For the top layer, those suitable include dupion, pure silk, velvet, cottons, fine wool, linen, crepe-backed satin. Choose good quality fabrics that are soft and fairly stretchy. Make sure the fabric is pressed carefully before use, as it is difficult to do this afterwards. Muslin is used for the backing. For the padding or interlining, use domette cotton or synthetic wadding, washed sheep's wool, or an old blanket.
Sewing threads Match the threads to the fabric where possible. Use Sylko, buttonhole twist, pure silk, stranded embroidery cottons, cotton perle, synthetic threads.
Needles Crewel or Sharps 7-9.
Stitches Running stitch, backstitch, chain stitch, machine stitch.

Design
Some of the traditional English quilting designs can be obtained in transfer form from craft and needlework shops. Those given in figs. 232 and 233 can be traced off the page, and transferred to the work. Consider also creating a modern original design using natural or geometric shapes, e.g. leaves, flowers, or indeed any suitable object around the home — plates, cups, saucers, etc. Draw round the shapes to make a pattern and combine them to make an attractive design for the article to be worked.

For a piece of work that is to be hand-quilted, trace the design onto the fabric

122

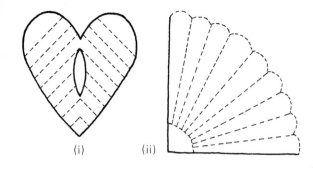

Fig. 232 Some quilting designs: (i) heart; (ii) fan; (iii) scallop shell; (iv) straight feather; (v) rose; (vi) tulip; (vii) cowslip leaf

using dressmaker's carbon paper. Alternatively, trace the design onto tissue paper and tack this onto the fabric. Make a running stitch round the design and tear away the paper. Work the quilting using the running stitches as a guide and remove them from the finished work.

Fig. 233 Some quilting designs for borders: (i) lined twist; (ii) chain; (iii) wineglass; (iv) straight feather; (v) hammock

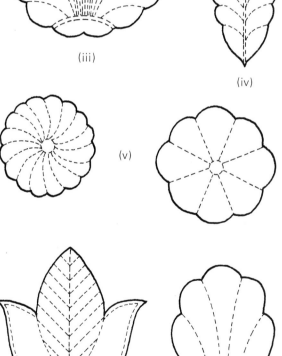

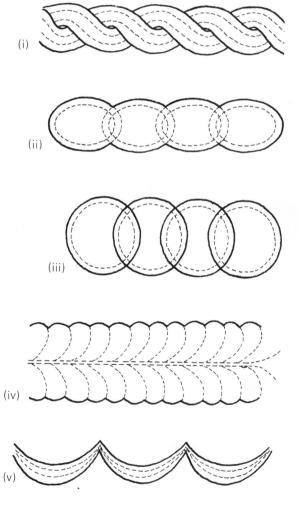

The design can also be marked by 'pricking' or scratching it onto the fabric using a blunt needle. Unfortunately, not all materials mark satisfactorily when this method is used, particularly some man-made fibres.

Making a quilted cushion cover
(a) Cut out the cushion fabric, muslin and interlining to the size required plus 2.5 cm (1 in.) turnings.
(b) Transfer or mark the design onto the right side of the cushion fabric (fig. 234).

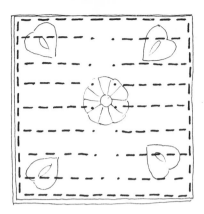

Fig. 235 **Cushion tacked up ready for quilting**

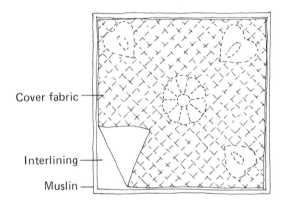

Cover fabric

Interlining

Muslin

Fig. 234 **Design marked out onto the face fabric**

(c) Place the muslin, interlining and cushion fabric with right sides uppermost. Smooth the fabric out and, starting from the centre, make a row of tacking stitches out to the edge of the fabric every 3.8 - 5 cm (1½-2 in.) across the work. Tack round the outer edge (fig. 235). Each piece of work needs to be prepared carefully using this method of tacking. The three layers of fabric need to be fixed securely together to prevent the work from moving and having a puckered effect when finished.
(d) Stitch round the design, using back-stitch, running stitch or chain stitch, or a combination of all three. Keep the stitching even and regular — the work should look as even on the back as on the front. Stitch the design from the centre of the work outwards through the three layers of fabric. If possible, the stitching should be worked using an embroidery frame.
(e) When all the quilting is complete, take out the tacking stitches and make up the cushion in the usual way.

When quilting a bedspread the design should be carefully positioned in the centre of the platform between the line of the pillow and the foot of the bed. The design could be repeated, or a complementary pattern made, for the rise over the pillows.

Some patterned fabrics can be most effective if quilted following the predominating lines of the design. This can be done either by hand or machine stitch and is a most effective form of decoration. It can be used most successfully for dressing table drapes, pelmets and other accessories for the home.

Finishing
The edges of quilting can be finished in three ways, depending on the article being made.
(i) Turn in the top edge and the backing fabric and work a line of running stitches as near to the edge as possible. Work a second row of stitches 0.6 cm (¼ in.) from the first.

124

(ii) Pipe the edge using crossway strip 2.5 - 3.8 cm (1-1½ in.) wide and a fine piping cord.

(iii) Bind the edges with crossway strip 3.8 cm (1½ in.) wide cut from the same fabric as the cover.

ITALIAN QUILTING

This type of quilting is purely decorative and can be worked by hand or machine using two layers of fabric. An interlining is not used as in English quilting, and therefore Italian quilting lacks the warmth afforded by the former method. Two rows of parallel stitching approximately 0.6 cm (¼ in.) apart are made to outline the design. A piece of quilting wool or thick yarn is then threaded through the channels to produce a raised effect. If a transparent fabric such as georgette or jap silk is used for the top layer, an attractive effect can be achieved by threading through coloured yarns or lurex threads. This is called shadow quilting.

Equipment
Fabrics Use fine linen, silk, satin, organdie, jap silk for the top layer and muslin for the backing.
Threads Match the threads to the fabrics. Sylko, buttonhole twist, pure silk, stranded embroidery cottons, synthetic threads.
Needles Crewel. Tapestry needle for threading through the yarns.
Stitches Running stitch, backstitch or machine stitch.

Design
Keep the patterns simple for Italian quilting, and not too close together or the pattern will be lost when the work is finished. For traditional work, double lines approximately 0.6 cm (¼ in.) apart are used, but these can be varied in width to suit modern designs and pieces of embroidery.

(a) Transfer the design to the right side of the top layer of fabric.

(b) Tack the muslin and the top layer together as for English quilting (fig. 235).

(c) Work the design through the two layers of fabric in running stitch, backstitch or machine stitch.

(d) Using a tapestry needle with a blunt point, thread the double line design with quilting wool, yarn or coloured threads. This is done from the back of the work, carefully inserting the needle between the muslin and the top layer of fabric, and gently pulling it through as the design permits. At any pronounced curve or sharp turn, take the needle back through the muslin to the back of the work and leave a small loop of the thread before inserting the needle back into the same hole (fig. 236). This prevents the work from pulling and the finished result will then be smooth and free from puckers.

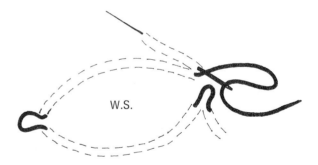

Fig. 236 **Leaving a loop at the back of the work in Italian quilting**

TRAPUNTO QUILTING

This type of quilting is used when larger areas of designs need to be padded. Synthetic fibre, kapok or cotton wool is inserted into the back of the work by slitting the muslin and stitching it together after padding.

(a) Transfer the design to the right side of the top layer.
(b) Tack the muslin and the top layer together as for English quilting (fig. 235).
(c) Work the design through the two layers of fabric using backstitch, running stitch or machine stitch.
(d) Slit the muslin at the back of the work where the design is to be padded and use a blunt needle to insert the filling. Close the opening securely with stitches (fig. 237).

Fig. 237 **Trapunto quilting, showing the design being padded and the opening stitched up**

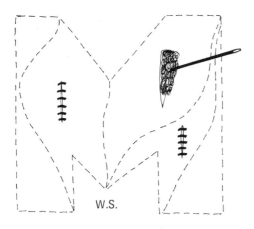

W.S.

14-Duvets and Traditional Quilts

DUVETS

The duvet, or continental quilt, is now probably the most popular form of bed covering throughout Europe, and has largely replaced the traditional down quilt or eider-down. Duvets appear to have gained in popularity for several reasons. They are less costly to use (as no other bed covering or blankets are necessary), they make bed-making extremely easy, they need no maintenance, and they are very light in weight.

Fillings

Duvets can be filled either with pure down or with synthetic fibres, and it is the quality of the filling that governs its price. Those fillings with pure goose or duck down are the most costly, but they do give the maximum warmth for the least possible weight. Down feathers come from the breasts of ducks and geese, and because they have no quills in them they are extremely light and resilient. It is the air that circulates round the down that provides the insulation and in turn the warmth; the better the quality of the down used, the less quantity is needed.

There are three types of fillings suitable for both duvets and traditional quilts — pure down, down and feather mixtures, and synthetics.

Pure down

Eider down   The eider duck is now so rare that its down is too costly to be used for household furnishings.

Goose down   This is the most luxurious of all economically viable fillings, as it provides the most warmth for its weight. White goose down is more costly than grey goose down, but there is little difference in their qualities.

Duck down   This is less expensive than goose down and probably represents the best value for money.

Down and feather mixtures

Down and feather   This is a mixture of down and feathers, and if labelled 'down and feather' must, in fact, contain more down than feathers, that is to say at least 51%.

Feather and down   This is also a mixture of feathers and down, but contains more feathers than down. The actual amount of down included can vary up to 49%.

Synthetic fillings

Terylene, Dacron and Courtelle are man-made fibres which are non-absorbent. As these are easily washable, this makes them an ideal filling for children's quilts or duvets. Synthetic fillings are available by weight (loose) or by the metre.

	Single size	*Double size*
Down	2-2½ lbs	3-3½ lbs
Down and feather*	2½-3 lbs	3½-4 lbs
Feather and down*	2½-3½ lbs	3½-4½ lbs
Synthetic filling	2½-3½ lbs	3½-4½ lbs

*this depends on the amount of down included.

Making a duvet

Materials

Use best-quality downproof cambric for constructing the outer cover of the duvet. This is a closely woven cotton fabric and is specially waxed to prevent the down from working through. It is available in widths from 90 to 140 cm (36 to 56 in.). The waxed or shiny side is the wrong side and must be placed next to the filling for it to be effective.

Always make sure the duvet is large enough for the bed and for the person using it. As a general guide the duvet should be made 46 cm (18 in.) wider than the width of the bed in order to allow it to hang over each side 15-23 cm (6-9 in.). The length of the duvet should be at least 2 m (6ft 6 in.); for an extra-long bed another 15 cm (6 in.) should be added, as this allows for a good overhang at the end of the bed. The most usual sizes are 1.37 x 2 m (54 x 78 in.) for a single, and 2.75 m x 2 m (81 x 78 in.) for a double. These can be adjusted to suit individual requirements.

A duvet needs a detachable cover to protect it and to keep it clean. Attractive ones can be made from easy-care fabrics and sheeting.

A duvet can be made like a large pillow, but it is considerably more effective in use if it is channelled down lengthwise and narrow gussets inserted. This ensures that the filling is evenly distributed and that it moves with the body.

	Single size duvet	Double size duvet
	1.37 m x 2 m (54 x 78 in.)	2.75 m x 2 m (81 x 78 in.)
Downproof cambric 140cm (56 in.) wide	4.2 m (4½ yds)	6 m (6¾ yds)
Lining sateen or calico	50 cm (½ yd.)	50 cm (½ yd.)

Making the outer cover

The following instructions are for making an outer cover for a single size duvet.

(a) From the lining sateen or calico cut and prepare four strips 3.8 cm (1½ in.) wide by 2 m (.78 in.) long, joining the fabric if necessary.

(b) Mark out the positions for the gussets on the wrong side of the cambric, i.e. the shiny waxed side (fig. 238).

(c) Pin and machine each gusset as shown in fig. 239, starting 2.5 cm (1 in.) from the top edge and finishing 2.5 cm (1 in.) from the centre fold line.

(d) Fold the right sides together along the centre fold line and pin and machine down one side of the duvet (fig. 240). Wax along the stitching with a piece of beeswax to avoid the down working through the holes made by the machine needle.

(e) With wrong side facing, take gusset strip 1 over the machined side seam and pin and tack to guide line 1 on the other side of the duvet, taking 0.6 cm (¼ in.) seam allowance. Machine into position.

(f) Take strip 2 and fold over and pin in the same way, matching to guide line 2. Tack and machine.

(g) Take strip 3 and match to guide line 3 in the same way. Tack and machine.

(h) Take strip 4 and match to guide line 4 in the same way. Tack and machine.

(i) To join the second side of the duvet, turn in the side edges 1.3 cm (½ in.) and machine stitch together on the right side 0.6 cm (¼ in.) from the edge. Make another row of machine stitching as close as possible to the first (fig. 241). Wax the stitching.

(j) Turn in and press a 1.3 cm (½ in.) seam allowance round the top edge of the duvet before inserting the filling.

The number of channels made can be varied to suit individual requirements, but it is usual to make 5 to 7 in a single size duvet and 7 to 9 in a double size.

Filling the duvet

(a) Work in a draught-free place — never outdoors.

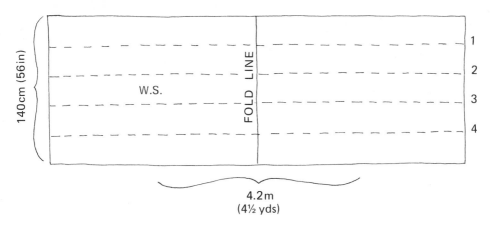

140cm (56in)

W.S.

FOLD LINE

1
2
3
4

4.2m
(4½ yds)

Fig. 238 **Positions for gussets marked on the wrong side of the cambric**

Fig. 239 **Gussets stitched in position**

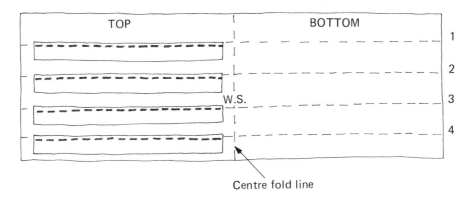

TOP   BOTTOM

1
2
3
4

W.S.

Centre fold line

(b) A single size duvet requires approximately 2½ lbs of down. Therefore, if five channels have been made each will need to be filled with approximately ½ lb. Divide the down into five equal quantities by putting it into five separate polythene bags, measuring the same width as the channel (approximately 23 cm (9 in.). The bags should be 30.5-35.5 cm (12-14 in.) deep.

(c) Insert one bag of down into each of the five channels open end first. Push it to the bottom of the channel and ease out the down. Remove the polythene bag.

(d) Close each channel with wooden clothes pegs as it is filled. When all channels are filled turn in 1.3 cm (½ in.) and tack the two top edges together.

(e) Make two rows of small machine stitching 0.6 cm (¼ in.) from the edge, and wax along the stitching.

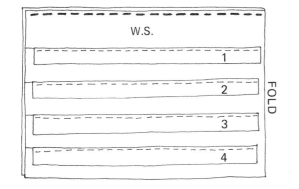

W.S.

1
2
3
4

FOLD

Fig. 240 **One side of the duvet stitched**

129

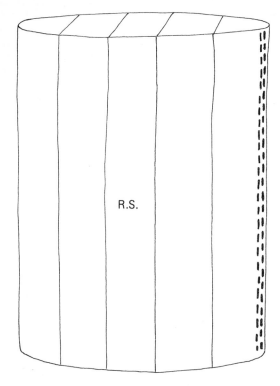

Fig. 241 **Second side of duvet stitched in position**

Duvet cover and pillowcase
Making the duvet cover

In order to keep a duvet clean and in good condition it is necessary to have a detachable cover that is easily washable. These covers are best made in polyester/cotton sheeting which is available in wide widths. Other lightweight easy care fabrics are also obtainable, but these are often only made in narrower widths, which necessitates more seaming.

The cover should not constrict the duvet when it is in use and so should ideally be made slightly larger than the duvet itself. Openings are usually made along the top edge of the cover and can be finished with press studs, touch fastening (such as Velcro), a zip, or a housewife flap can be made as in figs 243 to 246.

A duvet cover measuring approximately 205 cm x 140 cm (80 x 54 in.), requires 3 metres (3¼ yards) of fabric.

(a) Cut a strip of fabric approximately 215 cm (82 in.) wide x 3 m (120 in.) long (fig. 242).

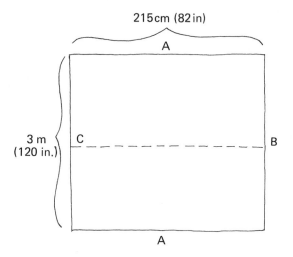

Fig. 242 **Cutting out duvet cover**

(b) At side C, which is the position for the opening, turn in and machine a 1.3 cm (½ in.) double hem to the wrong side of the fabric.

(c) With right sides of the fabric together, fold in half as in fig. 243 and machine up the two sides A and B using french seams.

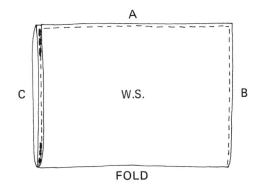

Fig. 243 **Duvet cover opening stitched up at side edges**

(d) At the opening edge, stitch up 7.5 cm (3 in.) at each side and apply a zip, touch fastening (such as Velcro) or snap fasteners, to close the opening.

Making the pillowcase

The following instructions are for making a pillowcase with a housewife-flap opening. Use plain or patterned sheeting to make a pillowcase 50 cm x 76 cm (19 x 30 in.).

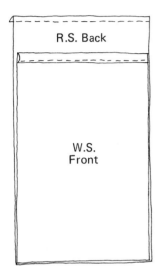

Fig. 244 **Hems stitched on pillowcase**

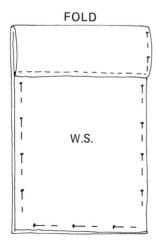

Fig. 245 **Front and back sections of pillowcase pinned in position**

(a) Cut out one piece of sheeting 51 x 96 cm (20 x 38 in.) for the front section of the pillowcase, and one piece of fabric 51 x 81 cm (20 x 32 in.) for the back section of the pillowcase.

(b) On the front section turn down a 2.5 cm (1 in.) double hem. On the back section turn down a 1.3 cm (½ in.) double hem (fig. 244).

(c) With right sides together, pin and tack the back and the front sections together as in fig. 245. Machine round three sides as in fig. 246. Clip corners. Turn right sides outside and press.

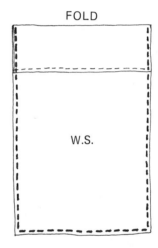

Fig. 246 **Pillowcase with housewife-style opening**

TRADITIONAL DOWN QUILTS

It is often much easier to make a new down quilt than to try and re-cover an old one. Very often the downproof cambric is worn and is no longer effective, and in this case it is advisable to start from scratch.

It is however, sometimes possible to use the filling from an old eiderdown. If it is a very old one it is quite possible that the down inside will be of a high quality. Check to make sure it does not contain any quills. Unpick the internal seams of the eiderdown and shake the down to one corner.

Fabrics

The quilt should be as light as possible, so choose a light-weight fabric such as silk, satin, seersucker, glazed cotton, sateen, etc. Brushed nylon could be used for the underside to avoid the quilt slipping off the bed. The quilt needs to be interlined with downproof cambric.

Fillings

Use the best quality filling to achieve a light-weight quilt, remembering that the better the quality the less of it is needed.

	Single size quilt	Double size quilt
Down	1½-2 lbs	2-2½ lbs
Down and feather	2-3 lbs	2½-3½ lbs
Feather and down	3-3½ lbs	3-4 lbs
Feathers	3½-4 lbs	4-5 lbs

Design

Choose a design for the quilt that suits the fabric, and keep it as simple as possible. Intricate designs present problems when the quilt is filled. Avoid narrow channels, less than 10 cm (4 in.) wide, and sharp angles, as this also makes filling difficult. Straight lines and curves are the easiest to work, and consideration must be given to the positioning of the 'leads' — that is the openings where the down will be inserted (fig. 247). It is important to make the filling as easy as possible, with the minimum number of leads to be sewn up when the quilt is complete. Mark out the design on a piece of graph paper and when a satisfactory one has been obtained draw a full-size quarter section to use as a pattern.

Making a single size down quilt

To make a down quilt for a single bed, the following materials are required: 4½ m (4½ yds) x 120 cm (48 in.) fabric for top and bottom sections of the cover; 4 m (4½ yds) x 120 cm (48 in.) wide downproof cambric

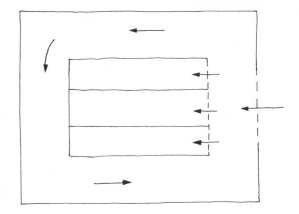

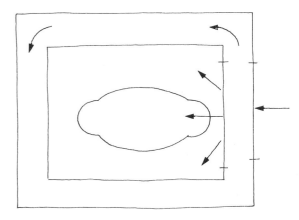

Fig. 247 **Designs showing 'leads' marked and the direction of the down filling**

for the interlining; 6 m (6½ yds) fine piping cord (Nos. 1 or 2).

(a) Cut two pieces of downproof cambric 2 m (65 in.) long and 1 m (40 in.) wide for the interlining. This allows for approximately 10 cm (4in.) each way to be taken up when the quilt is filled.

(b) For the top and bottom sections of the top cover cut two pieces of light-weight fabric the same size as the interlining.

(c) On the wrong side (i.e. the shiny waxed side) of one piece of cambric, mark out the design with a pencil or tailor's chalk, using the paper pattern as a guide.

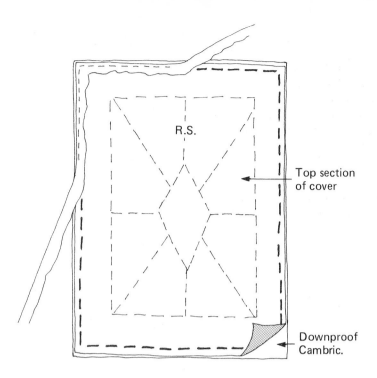

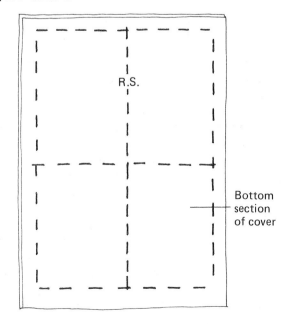

(d) Place the right side of the cambric to the wrong side of the top section of the cover fabric and tack the two pieces together round the outer edges (fig. 248).

(e) Following the design marked on the wrong side of the cambric, tack through both layers of fabric to the top section.

(f) Make and apply an edge trimming to the right side of the top section of the cover (fig. 248). This could be a piped or ruched edge (see page 34).

(g) Tack the wrong side of the bottom section of the cover to the right side of the second piece of downproof cambric as in fig. 249, but do not mark the design on this side.

(h) With the two right sides of the quilt cover facing, tack and machine as for a cushion round the three sides, leaving a 30.5 cm (12 in.) opening at one of the short ends. Turn right sides out.

(i) Tack through the four thicknesses of fabric on the design lines, but leave the

Fig. 248 **Design tacked through downproof cambric to the top section of the cover**

Fig. 249 **Bottom section of cover tacked to downproof cambric**

133

leads untacked so that the down can be easily inserted.

(j) Machine stitch through all thicknesses on the design lines, leaving the leads open.

Filling the quilt

(a) If using new down to fill the quilt, use an old pillowcase which has been opened at both ends. Stitch one end of the pillowcase to the new quilt at the 30.5 cm (12 in.) opening, and insert a bag of down (fig. 250). Make sure that the open end of the pillowcase is firmly

Fig. 250 **Filling a down quilt**

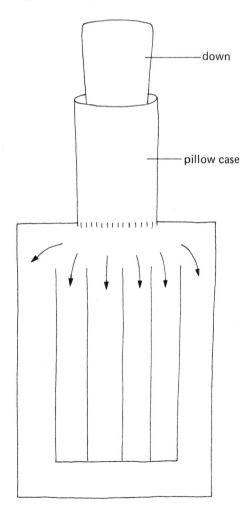

secured (with string or clothes pegs) before putting the down into the new quilt. Continue in this way until the quilt is satisfactorily filled and the down evenly distributed. Pin down each lead in turn as each section is filled.

(b) Remove the pillowcase from the new quilt and pin and tack the opening carefully. Slipstitch firmly together by hand.

(c) Tack the leads down and machine or backstitch by hand.

Making a double size down quilt

A double size quilt for a bed 1.3 metres (54 in.) wide would be cut 1.5 m x 1.7 m (59 in. x 67 in.) If a wide enough fabric is not available it may be necessary to join the widths together. It is advisable to incorporate these joins in the overall design of the quilt and so a border should be made to go round the central panel. This means that each corner of the border must be carefully mitred (fig. 251).

(a) Plan the design as for the single size quilt and cut out the central panel to the required size.

(b) For the border section cut a piece of fabric the length of the quilt and the width required. Divide it into four equal strips. The border can vary in width from 20.5 cm - 30.5 cm (8-12 in.) and can be made to suit the individual design.

(c) Pin and tack the border sections to the central panel and mitre the corners as in figs 57-60. Machine the mitred corners and press the seams open.

(d) Machine the borders to the central panel, pressing the seams open, then proceed as for the single size quilt.

QUILTS WITH SYNTHETIC FILLINGS

This type of quilt is made using a different method from the one used for traditional

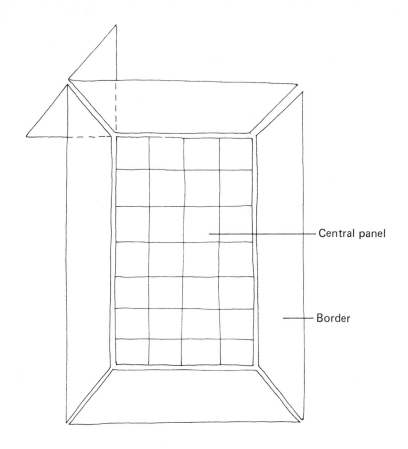

Fig. 251 **Planning a double size down quilt**

down quilts, as it is not possible to insert the filling after the cover is made. Ready made Terylene pads can be obtained in various sizes from cot to double bed size, or the loose synthetic fibre can be bought by weight, spread out to the required thickness, and covered with a muslin backing. About 1½ lbs is usually enough for a single size quilt and 2½ lbs will probably be required for a double size.

Fabrics

As Terylene is completely washable, choose a drip-dry non-iron fabric for the quilt cover. An interlining is not necessary for this type of quilt. Brushed nylon is a good choice for the bottom section as it does not slip. Enough fabric is needed to cover both sides of the quilt, together with an edge trimming, e.g. a ruched or piped edge.

Design

Plan a simple all-over design which will keep the pad of fibre firmly in position. Straight or diagonal lines (squares or diamonds) are ideal for this purpose. Make a pattern on paper and mark out as for a down quilt.

Making the quilt

(a) Cut out the fabric for the top and bottom of the cover to the size of the pad plus 1.3 cm - 2.5 cm (½ - 1 in.) turnings all round. Cut a piece of muslin the same size if using loose synthetic fibre.

(b) Lay the Terylene pad or loose fibre to the wrong side of the top section and place the piece of muslin on top. Pin and tack round the outer edge.

135

(c) From the right side of the top section pin and tack the design through to the muslin, using contrasting coloured thread (fig. 252).

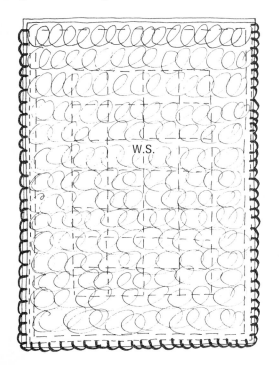

W.S.

(d) Make an edge trimming, e.g. a gathered ruche or piped edge, and apply this by pinning and tacking to the right side of the top section of the cover. If using piping cord make sure that it is a nylon one so that it has the same washing qualities as the quilt.

(e) Machine stitch the trimming in place along one short side where the opening will be positioned.

(f) Place the right side of the bottom section to the right side of the top section and tack and machine the three sides, leaving the opening unstitched. Blanket stitch the Terylene to the three sides and along the opening edge (fig. 252).

(g) Turn the quilt to the right side and slipstitch the opening.

(h) Tack the design through all thicknesses of the quilt. Machine stitch the design using a fine needle, using a large straight or zigzag stitch, taking care not to pucker the work underneath. Alternatively the design can be worked by hand using a stab stitch. Remove all tackings.

15·Lampshades

Lampshades play an important part in the overall decor of a room. They are functional as well as decorative, and have the advantage of being less costly to make than most other items of soft furnishings. They are probably changed more frequently for this reason, and a room can be given a new lease of life with one or two fresh lampshades.

A lampshade demands a high standard of workmanship and meticulous attention to detail, because as soon as the lampshade is lit, any defects will immediately become apparent.

Choose fabrics for lampshades carefully, taking into consideration colour, texture and quality. Try to match the line of the lampshade frame to that of the base so that the two together present a pleasing design. Relate the size of the frame to the base so that a good overall balance is achieved. Choose a base that is solid enough to be practical in use, remembering that it is often easier to choose a frame for a base with simple lines than for one with overall detail.

EQUIPMENT

It is not necessary to have any special tools for making lampshades, but the following basic equipment will be found useful.

Needles
Use Sharps 3-9 for making soft lampshades and Betweens 5/6 for firm lampshades.

Pins
Best quality steel dressmaking pins should be used, making sure that they are free from rust. Glass-headed pins can be used, but as they are extremely sharp extra care is needed when using them. Blood can be removed from fabric by chewing a piece of tacking thread and rubbing it gently on the bloodstain. This removes the stain without leaving a water mark.

Lampshade tape
Lampshade tape or soft cotton tape, 1.3 cm (½ in.) wide, to bind the lampshade frame. Lampshade tape is a poor-quality unbleached tape which is loosely woven. When the frame has been taped it can be dipped into a cold water dye to match the colour of the lining if necessary (e.g. on a tiffany style lampshade where the struts will show).

Adhesive
A good, quick-drying, all-purpose adhesive (such as UHU) is necessary when making firm lampshades. This is also useful when applying some trimmings to soft lampshades where stitching is not satisfactory (e.g. velvet ribbon, crossway strip).

Clothes pegs
Wooden clip-on clothes pegs are required for making firm lampshades.

Trimmings
There are many good commercial trimmings available, but very attractive ones can also be made by hand.

FRAMES AND FITTINGS

When buying a lampshade frame, choose one that is made from copper wire if possible. The frame should be firm and the joints strong. The wire should be of a suitable gauge or thickness for the size of the frame and should enable it to support the fabric firmly. If necessary, file down any rough edges at the joints and paint it with a quick drying enamel paint, making sure it is quite hard before taping.

Sometimes it is possible to use an old frame, especially if it is particularly well made and not out of shape, and is of a pleasing design. The old binding tape should be removed and the frame checked for rust. File it down if necessary and paint it in the usual way.

Fig. 254 **Butterfly clip for small shades and wall lights**

Fig. 255 **Oval drum with dropped pendant fitting. Suitable for both hanging shades and table lamps**

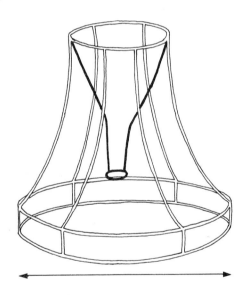

Fig. 253 **Adjustable gimbal fitting on curved empire frame, showing diameter measurement of frame**

Frames are made in various sizes from 7.5 cm - 10 cm (3 - 4 in.) to 51-56 cm (20-22 in.). This measurement is usually taken across the diameter of the base ring of the frame (see fig. 253). Make sure that the correct fitting for the lamp is chosen. Examples of these are given in figs 253 - 262. When an unusual shape or size is required, it is sometimes possible to have a frame made especially to order.

Lampshades fall into two groups — soft fabric shades and firm rigid ones. Soft fabric lampshades are made from flexible materials — silks, satins, lawns, chiffons, cottons, etc. It is essential to make these on frames that have struts as well as a ring at the top and bottom, as it is these that give the frame its shape.

138

Firm lampshades are made from stiff or rigid materials, such as buckram, parchment and covered card. When making a firm shade a ring set is used. This consists of a top and bottom ring with the appropriate fitting. Frames with struts can also be used, but they are not essential, as the rigid materials form the shape of the shade.

Fig. 258 **Duplex fitting used on a large bowed shade with a collar**

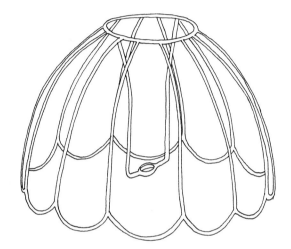

Fig. 256 **Adjustable gimbal fitting on a tiffany-style lampshade**

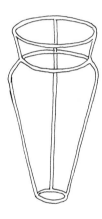

Fig. 259 **Shade carrier or support for use with shades having duplex fittings**

SOFT LAMPSHADES

Choice of fabrics for cover and lining
There are so many dress and furnishing fabrics available that there is really no limit to the choice. When choosing fabrics, bear in mind the following points and do not be afraid to experiment with new fabrics as they become available, provided they appear to have the qualities necessary.

Fig. 257 **Pendant fitting on a tiffany style lampshade**

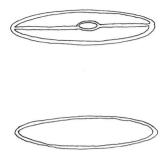

Fig. 260 **Ring set used for making firm lampshades**

(1) Use fabric that has plenty of 'give' or elasticity. Fabric that stretches well will mould easily to the shape of the frame without wrinkling. Stiff, non-stretchy fabrics are not suitable for curved frames. Crêpe-backed satin, rayon dupions, silk shantung, and wild silk are examples of suitable fabrics for making tailored shades.

(2) Materials that split and tear easily are not suitable (for example, taffeta, rayon and satin lining fabric) as these show all pin marks and also do not wash well.

Fig. 261 **Straight-sided empire shade with pendant fitting for hanging shades**

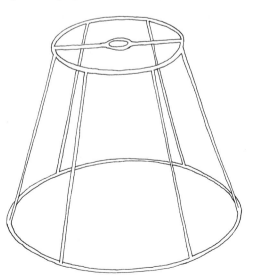

(3) Avoid using · heavy furnishing fabrics, as besides being difficult to work, very little light will filter through and the shade is likely to be too opaque.

(4) Dress cottons, ginghams, broderie Anglaise, lace and lawn are particularly suitable for tiffany style lampshades, and attractive effects can also be achieved by using coloured linings with these fabrics.

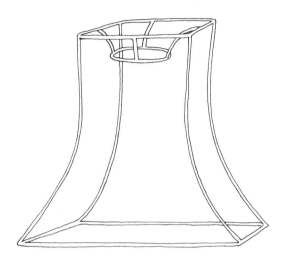

Fig. 262 **Sectional shade with duplex fitting**

(5) When making pleated or swathed lampshades, choose fabric with good draping qualities, such as silk chiffon or georgette. Nylon chiffon is not suitable as it does not pleat and set well as it is too springy.

(6) Always use crêpe-backed satin for lining soft lampshades. This fabric stretches well and it is easy to use. It gives body to the shade when using light-weight fabrics for the cover, and because of its shiny surface it reflects the light well. Crêpe-backed satin is available in a wide range of colours and can also be used for the lampshade cover, using either the crêpe or the shiny side. Most lampshades are enhanced by a lining.

140

(7) Any colour is acceptable for a lamp-shade provided it fits into the scheme of the room. However, some colours give a more attractive light than others. These include tones of gold and red. Blue transmits a cold light; browns and greens can be most effective, but can give a dingy light, so care is needed when choosing both the cover fabric and the lining. Dead white shades give a cold light, but can be enhanced by a lining of pink or peach. Before buying lampshade fabrics, test them over a lighted bulb to see the effects produced. Remember that a coloured lining can dramatically change the tone of the outer cover, and can also be used to add warmth to a 'cool' colour.

(8) Most soft lampshades can be washed when necessary. It is important that the shade is dried as quickly as possible to avoid rust forming on the frame, so choose a good drying day and wash gently in warm water using a mild detergent. Rinse thoroughly and hang on the line to drip dry. When dry, put in an airing cupboard for 24 hours, as this helps the fabric to tighten up on the frame and ensures that it is perfectly dry. If a contrasting coloured trimming has been used check the colour fastness of this, as it could run and spoil the shade.

Taping the frame

This is the most important process as it is essential to provide a firm foundation for the pinning and stitching of the fabric. The binding tape needs to be firm, smooth and tight on all the struts and the rings. If it is at all loose the stitching will slip, and a disappointing shade will result. Use 1.3 cm (½ in.) wide lampshade tape or soft cotton tape. For the struts allow approximately one and a half times the length of each strut. If more is allowed the tape will become too bulky. For the top and bottom rings allow twice the circumference. More is needed for the rings as the tape is bound round each joint of the strut and ring.

Tape each strut separately and then tape the top and bottom rings. Always start and finish at a joint in the strut and ring, to avoid the tape working loose. No sewing is necessary except where taping rings for firm lampshades where there are no struts. A small piece of adhesive tape can be used to hold the tape in position when starting. Finish off by sewing on the outside of the ring so that when the material is applied to the ring it covers the stitches.

(a) Place the tape under the ring, starting at the top of the frame. Tuck in and wind the tape round the strut just overlapping it. This is done at rather an acute angle and is helped if a slight pull is given at each time round. This stretches the tape slightly and makes it mould to the strut easily. Keep the tape smooth and taut and avoid any ridges that may appear (figs. 263 and 264).

(b) At the bottom of the strut turn the lampshade to the position in fig. 265 and wind the tape round the bottom ring, taking it first to the left and then to the right of the ring (a figure of eight). Finish off with a knot as in fig. 266 and pull tightly. Trim off the end to the bottom ring.

(c) Tape each strut in this way and then tape the top and bottom rings making a figure of eight round each joint in the strut and ring. Finish off as before.

Curved empire lampshade with a balloon lining

This method is one of the quickest and most satisfactory methods of making lampshades. It can be used for many shades provided the measurement round the middle, or smallest part of the frame, is not more than the top ring. For frames with an accentuated waist it is safer to work them in two or

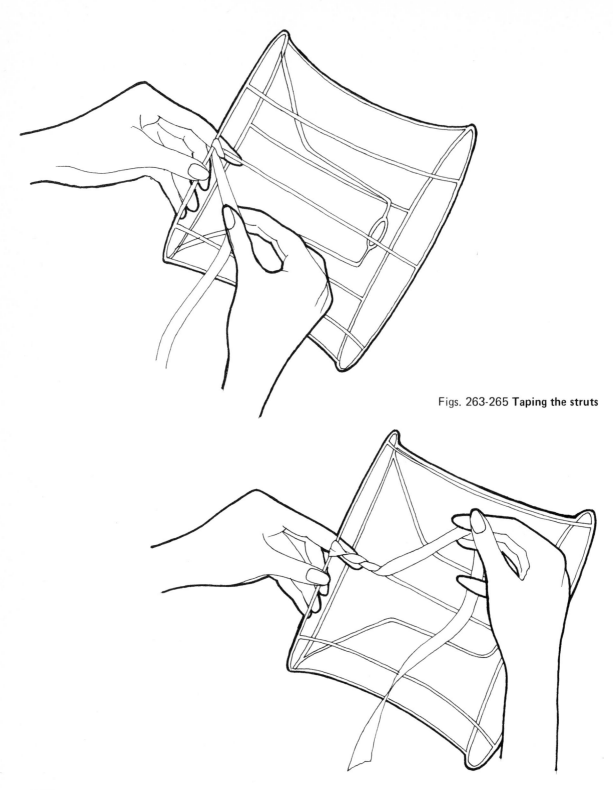

Figs. 263-265 **Taping the struts**

more sections, depending on their design and size. However, if the measurement of the 'waist' does not vary very greatly from that of the top ring, this method can safely be used, provided the fabric has plenty of give, and the fabric is worked on the cross grain instead of the straight grain.

A rough estimate of the fabric needed can be obtained by measuring the depth of one strut plus 10 cm (4 in.), and the circumference of the bottom ring plus 12.5 cm (5 in.).

(a) Tape the frame.

(b) Fold the cover fabric in half with the right sides together. Place onto one side of the frame only with the fold at the top edge. Place a pin in each corner to hold the fabric together. The material is placed onto the frame on the straight of the grain with the selvedge running from the top to the bottom of the frame (fig. 267).

(c) Place a pin at ABC and D pinning just into the top of the tape and not behind the back of the frame.

(d) Pin the fabric to the two side struts AC and BD placing pins at 2.5 cm (1 in.) intervals. Do not pin at the top and bottom rings until most of the fulness has been taken to the sides. (Always place pins on the side struts with the heads facing the centre of the shade. Pins on the top and bottom rings should face towards the centre. This reduces the risk of damaging clothes and body).

(e) Tighten the fabric to the top and bottom rings to remove wrinkles, pinning every 2.5 cm (1 in.).

(f) Complete pinning on the side struts, inserting pins first at 1.3 cm (½ in.) intervals and then finally at 0.6 cm (¼ in.) intervals.

(g) With a pencil, carefully mark over the pins on the side struts, extending the line 1.3 cm (½ in.) above A and B and C and D, and extending the pencil mark 1.3 cm (½ in.) round the top and bottom rings at ABC and D (fig. 268).

143

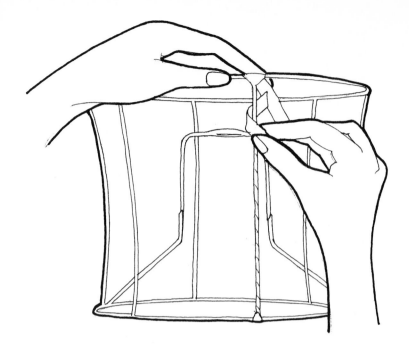

Fig. 266 **Making a figure of eight at the lower edge of the strut**

Fig. 267 **Placing fabric correctly on the frame with selvedges running downwards**

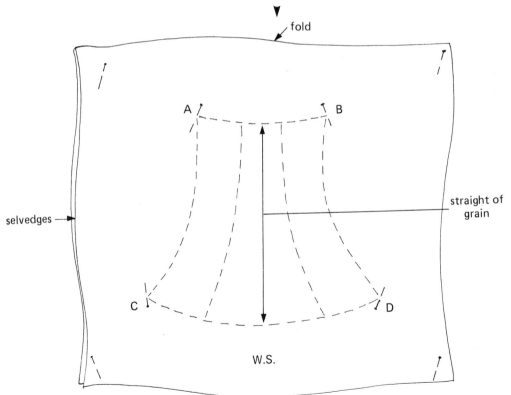

fold

A   B

straight of
grain

selvedges →

C   D

W.S.

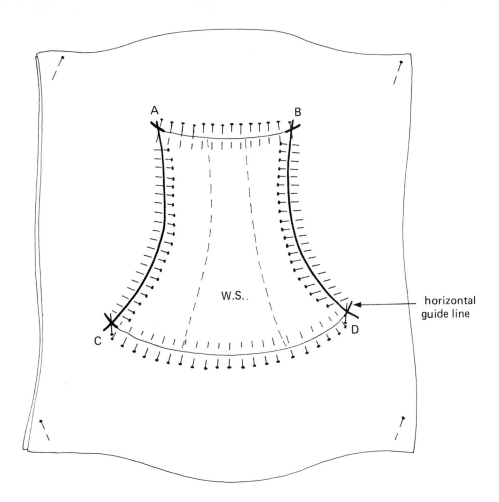

Fig. 268 **Taking out fullness and pinning fabric to side struts; seam line and horizontal guide lines at top and bottom rings are marked with a pencil**

(h) Leaving the corner pins in to hold the fabric together, take out all the pins from the frame. Machine down the pencil line from the top to the bottom, using a medium-sized stitch, and stretching the fabric very slightly while machining. This avoids the stitches breaking when the cover is stretched over the top of the frame.

(i) Trim seams to 0.6 cm (¼ in.) at each side and cut along the fold line at the top edge (fig. 269).

(j) Prepare the lining in the same way and set aside.

Applying the cover

(a) Press the cover keeping the fabric flat — do not press the seams open.

(b) Slip the cover over the frame with the right side outside. Make sure that the seams are placed on the side struts with the seams behind the strut. Match the horizontal pencil lines at the top and bottom rings.

(c) Pin round the top and bottom rings of the lampshade, gradually tightening the fabric. Place pins at 2.5 cm (1 in.) intervals (fig. 270) making sure that they are placed so that they avoid damage to clothes and body.

145

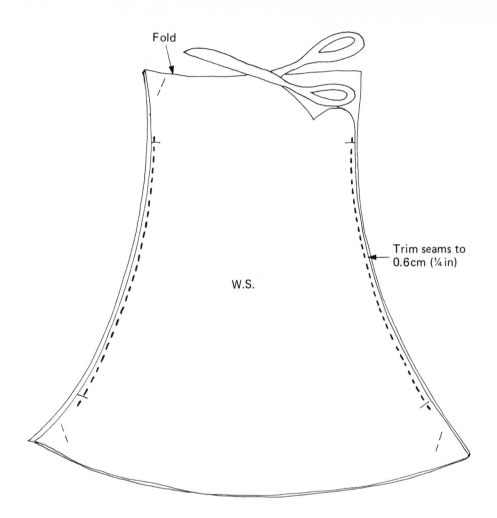

Fold

W.S.

Trim seams to
0.6cm (¼ in)

Fig. 269 **Cutting along fold line at top of fabric**

(d) Oversew the cover to the frame using a short length of double matching thread. Do not use a long piece of thread as this will catch round the pins. The stitches should be on the outside edge of the top and bottom rings, and the stitches should be worked from right to left.

(e) Cut away surplus fabric from the top and bottom of the lampshade trimming close up to the stitches. If this material is not cut away very close to the stitching it will make a bulky finish when the lining is inserted (fig. 271).

Applying the balloon lining

(a) Press the lining flat and do not press the seams open. Drop the lining into the shade matching the seams and horizontal pencil marks at the top and bottom rings.

(b) Pin the lining to the top and bottom rings, making sure that the pins are placed on the outside edge of the shade. Adjust the lining by tightening the pins at the top and bottom of the shade until the lining is taut and smooth and all fullness has been disposed of (fig. 272).

(c) When pinning the lining round the top ring, unpick the seam down to the horizontal pencil mark and spread out

146

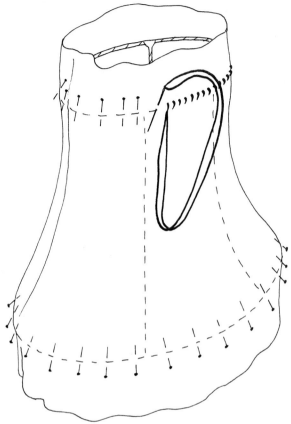

Fig. 270 **Oversewing cover to frame, showing position of stitches**

the material to enable the lining to fit neatly round the gimbal fitting (fig. 273).

(d) Oversew the lining to the frame using matching thread in the same way as the outer cover. The stitches should be on the outer edge of the lampshade so that they are covered completely when. the trimming is applied.

Neatening the gimbal fitting

From a piece of lining fabric, cut a piece of crossway strip 10 cm (4 in.) long and 2.5 cm (1 in.) wide. Fold in three to make a strip 1.3 cm (½ in.) wide. Press. Slip under the gimbal fitting and pin in position as in fig. 274. Oversew securely in place on the stitching line for the lining, keeping the stitches well down onto the outside of the shade.

Fig. 271 **Cutting away surplus fabric close to stitching at bottom ring**

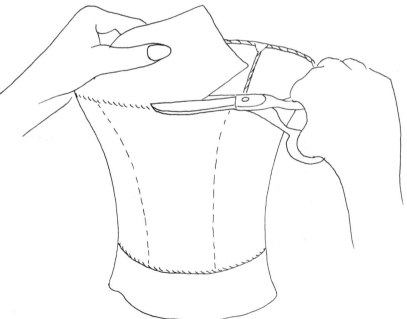

147

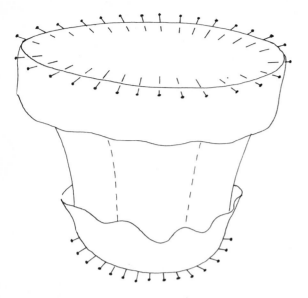

Fig. 272 **Lining pinned into position at top and bottom rings**

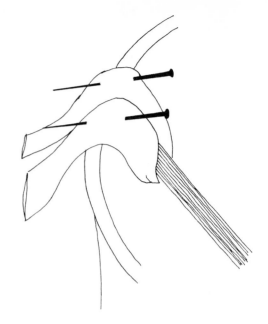

Fig. 274 **Neatening gimbal fitting**

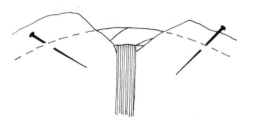

Fig. 273 **Pinning lining round gimbal fitting**

Trimmings

A trimming is used to cover stitches and sometimes seams, but it must also serve to decorate and complement the finished lampshade. Careful consideration should therefore be given to the texture of the fabric and the style of the shade, as well as to the base on which it will stand. Remember to keep silky braids and fringes for soft silky shades, and use thicker, more coarsely woven trimmings, such as piping cord, cotton braids, ricrac braids, etc. for firm lampshades; these more closely match the rough texture of perhaps buckram or hessian.

Although there is a wide range of attractive commercially made trimmings available, in many widths and styles, it is not always easy to match colours exactly. If colours cannot be matched, and a contrast is not possible, gold metallic braids and laces can be used; they work well with many colours and can also be used successfully with some hand-made trimmings (e.g. crossway strip).

Hand-made trimmings can be made using crochet, tatting or macramé techniques, or by plaiting braids, wools or rushes in various thicknesses. Velvet ribbon can be most effective when gathered and applied to the top and bottom edges. Machine embroidery can also be used to advantage to make scalloped edges. A petal-edged ruching can be made by working diagonal rows of small running stitches on a folded crossway strip (figs. 275-277).

A trimming should always be sewn onto the shade unless a more even effect can be achieved by using an adhesive, e.g. when using narrow velvet ribbon, russia braid or crossway strip.

148

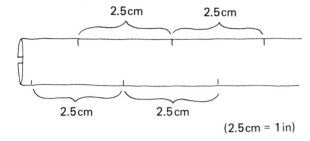

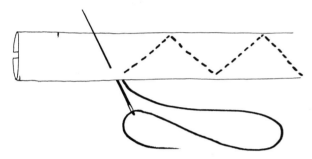

(2.5 cm = 1 in)

Fig. 275 **Marking points for petal-edged ruching**

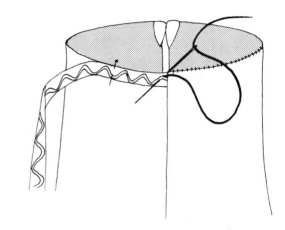

Fig. 276 **Running stitches worked through marking points**

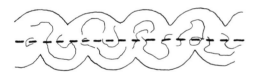

Fig. 277 **Finished effect of gathering stitches on petal-edged ruching**

Measure very accurately the circumference of the top and bottom rings to estimate the amount of trimming required. Add 5 cm (2 in.) to each measurement. This allows 1.3 cm (½ in.) turnings and a little extra to enable the trimming to be eased onto the shade. When a fringe of any type is being used, take care not to stretch it when sewing it onto the shade, as this will pull it to the inside of the bottom ring and it will not hang well.

When applying trimmings make sure that the two joins at the top and bottom of the lampshade are made on the same side of the shade.

Braids and fringes

To sew on the trimming, fold in the end 1.3 cm (½ in.). Starting at a side strut, pin on the trimming and sew as in fig. 278 and 279 using a zigzag stitch. Take care that the stitching does not go through to the inside of the shade. Finish by turning in the end of the trimming 1.3 cm (½ in.), and butting the ends together at the side strut.

Velvet ribbons

As these lack elasticity and will not mould easily to a curve, they are best stretched onto the shade and applied with an adhesive. Butt the ends together at the side strut.

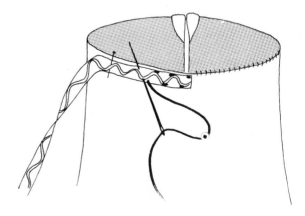

Figs. 278 and 279 **Sewing on the trimming**

149

Crossway strip

Prepare enough crossway strip 2.5 cm (1 in.) wide to fit round the top and bottom of the shade. Fold into three, and make a strip approximately 1.3 cm (½ in.) wide. When attaching to the shade apply the end of the strip to the outside edge of the lampshade, starting 0.6 cm (¼ in.) beyond a side strut. Use a small knife to apply the adhesive, and spread it evenly and carefully over the strip a little at a time. Press gently to the shade to achieve a perfectly even finish. The strip should just cover the oversewing stitches, but should not extend to the inside of the shade. To finish off, turn in 0.6 cm (¼ in.) at the end of the strip, secure with a little adhesive, and apply over the other end (fig. 280). This trimming can also be used very successfully to cover seams on tiffany and other styles of shades.

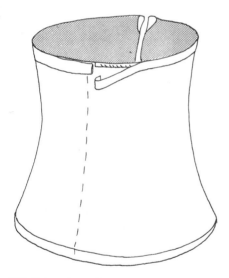

Fig. 280 **Trimming a lampshade with crossway strip; the two joins of the trimming are on the same side of the shade**

Tiffany-style lampshades

Tiffany lampshades blend well with traditional and modern furnishing schemes and look effective in bathrooms, kitchens, bedrooms and dining rooms. They can be treated in many different ways and look equally effective whether made in coarse linen or dainty lawn. They look well made up in fabric to match the curtains or wallpaper in the room.

There are two methods of covering a tiffany-style lampshade. The first, which is simple and fairly quick to do, consists of making a tube with a casing at the top and bottom through which elastic is threaded. A lining is not used and the cover can be removed for washing.

The second method consists of tailoring the lampshade, and takes longer as the fabric is sewn onto the frame in sections. An external lining is used, as a balloon lining is not practicable for this shape of frame.

Tiffany-style frames vary considerably in shape, so buy one that is suitable for the method chosen.

Gathered tiffany lampshade with a frill

This is suitable for light-weight fabrics only and those that have good draping qualities, e.g. lace, voile, lawn and light dress cottons (fig. 281). Heavier fabrics are best made up using the second method.

(a) Prepare and tape the frame. It is not necessary to tape the struts but they must be painted.

Fig. 281 **Tiffany lampshade made in the gathered style**

150

(b) A rectangle of fabric is needed which should be the length of the circumference of the bottom ring, plus 10 cm (4 in.). The width should be the measurement of the strut plus 7.5 cm (3 in.). If it is necessary to join the fabric to obtain the required length, cut two pieces of equal size.

(c) Join the fabric with a french seam to make a tube. Press the seam flat.

(d) To make the casing at the top and bottom edge, turn over 1.3 cm (½ in.) and press, then turn over another 1.3 cm (½ in.) and press. Machine along top and bottom edges of casing, leaving 1.3 cm (½ in.) open for inserting elastic (fig. 282).

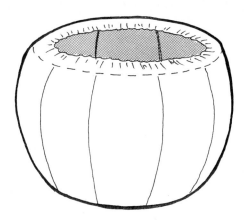

Fig. 283 Marking position of frill with line of tacking stitches

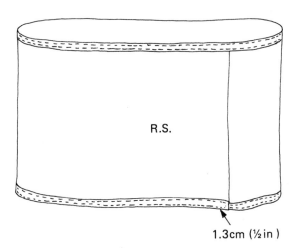

1.3cm (½ in)

Fig. 282 Casing machine stitched leaving 1.3 cm (½ in.) for elastic

(e) Insert a narrow tape or piece of string into the casing at top and bottom and slip onto the frame. Adjust tape to fit and mark to get the length of elastic required.

(f) Mark position of frill with tailor's chalk or tacking thread. This is the fitting line (fig. 283).

(g) Take off shade and insert required length of elastic, sewing the ends firmly together.

(h) To make the frill, cut a strip of fabric on the straight grain of the material 10-15 cm (4-6 in.) wide and one and a half times the circumference of the bottom ring. Join the ends of the strip together with a narrow french seam.

(i) Fold in half lengthwise and turn in raw edges 1.3 cm (½ in.) at top edge. Run a row of running stitches along the fabric 1.3 cm (½ in.) from the top. Gather up the frill and adjust to fit the bottom of the lampshade.

(j) Apply the frill to the cover along the fitting line (fig. 284).

Fig. 284 The frill tacked onto the lampshade

151

Tailored tiffany lampshade

A variety of fabrics can be used when making this type of lampshade as the material is stretched onto the frame on the cross of the grain in four separate sections. Suitable fabrics include broderie Anglaise, silks, dupions and light furnishing cottons, which may be plain, patterned or textured. Avoid using fabrics with pronounced stripes as these are difficult to match successfully.

Do not use a frame that has a very marked convex curve at the top and bottom (see fig. 257) as this type usually has too many struts, and is more successful when used for the gathered style.

Because of the shape of the frame, a balloon lining is not practical for a tailored tiffany lampshade, so an external lining is fitted to the frame before the top cover is applied.

(a) Prepare and tape the frame.

(b) About ½ to ¾ metre (20in - 30 in.) of both cover and lining fabric is usually sufficient for most sizes of this style of shade. To obtain an accurate estimate, measure the size of one quarter of the frame and make a rough paper pattern, allowing generous turnings all round of approximately 7.5 cm (3 in.). Four pieces of fabric this size will need to be cut on the cross grain of the fabric. If patterns need to be centralized or matched, more fabric would of course be needed.

(c) Place the lining fabric over a quarter of the frame on the cross of the grain (fig. 285) placing pins at A B C and D to hold the fabric to the frame. Pin to the top and bottom rings along AB and CD and down the two struts AC and BD, easing out any fullness.

(d) When all the fullness has been disposed of and the fabric is smooth and taut, oversew the fabric to the frame using matching thread. Start sewing at B, continue along to A then to C D and back to B (fig. 285).

(e) Trim away surplus fabric from the two struts AC and BD. At the top and bottom rings AB and CD trim off to leave 5 cm (2 in.) of fabric for neatening the edges (fig. 286).

(f) Apply the lining to the other three quarters of the frame in the same way.

Fig. 285 and 286 **Oversewing fabric to frame leaving 5 cm (2 in.) of fabric at top and bottom for neatening edges**

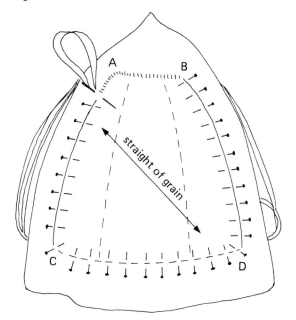

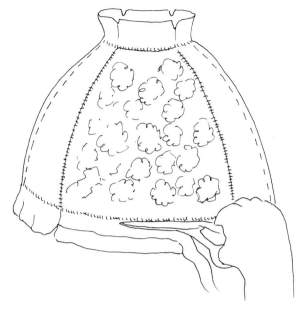

Fig. 287 **Trimming surplus fabric away close to stitching**

(g) When the lining has been completed apply the top cover in the same way, using the same struts for stitching. Trim the top and bottom rings of the cover close to the stitching (fig. 287).

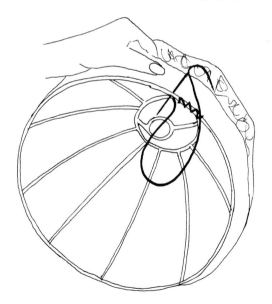

Fig. 288 **Stitching back fabric to neaten edge**

(h) To neaten the top and bottom rings, fold back the lining fabric over the top cover and stitch back as in fig. 288. Trim close to stitches.

(i) Neaten the stitches on the struts by trimming with crossway strip (see page 150).

(j) The top and bottom rings can be trimmed with decorative braid or fringe, or can be finished with a crossway strip.

Pleated and swathed lampshade

These can be made using either straight or diagonal pleats, or a combination of both. Attractive effects can also be obtained with 'sunray' and 'fan' pleating. A certain amount of care and patience is needed when making these more advanced lampshades if a professional result is to be achieved. Their success lies in accurate pleating and attractive colour combinations. Some ideas for pleated lampshades are shown in fig. 289.

Choose soft sheer fabrics with good draping qualities such as silk or rayon chiffon and georgette. Nylon is not suitable as it does not pleat and set satisfactorily. Silk shantung can be used for straight pleating, but is not fine enough for the swathed styles.

Select the motif for sunray pleating with care, as this is the central focal point. A handmade motif can be most attractive, but make sure that it is a perfect piece of work. Guipure lace, decorative buttons, beadwork and embroidery can all be used to advantage.

Straight-pleated lampshade

(a) Choose a frame that has straight, not curved, sides or struts.

(b) Prepare and tape the frame.

(c) To estimate the amount of fabric, measure the circumference of the bottom ring and multiply by three to obtain the width, then measure the depth of the frame and add 5 cm (2 in.) to obtain the length.

(d) Prepare and make the lining as on page 141. An external lining is used on a pleated shade instead of a balloon lining

153

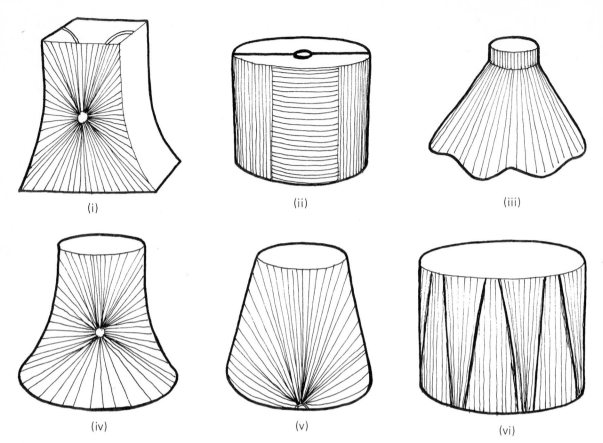

Fig. 289 (i) Sectional lampshade showing sunray pleating used on one section; (ii) oval drum lampshade worked with horizontal and vertical pleating; (iii) straight pleated lampshade with collar (iv) sunray pleating with central motif worked on empire shaped frame; (v) straight-sided empire shape worked in sunray pleating with motif positioned at lower edge; (vi) fan pleating used on a drum shade

so that the pleating is not disturbed when it has been worked. Place the prepared lining over the top of the lampshade frame on the outside of the struts, and pin as in fig. 290. At the bottom ring make a slash at each strut, fold in lining 3 mm (1/8 in.), and pin onto the front of the bottom ring as in fig. 290. Oversew the top and bottom rings in the usual way.

(e) Trim the lining to the stitching at the bottom ring, but at the top ring trim off

to leave 2.5 cm (1 in.) for neatening the edge after the pleating has been worked.

Working the pleats

(a) Tear or cut the fabric into strips the depth required. This should be done across the fabric from selvedge to selvedge so that the grain runs from the top to the bottom of the lampshade. The pleating will then set well. Cut off all selvedges.

(b) Decide on the width of the pleat and whether or not a space is required between each pleat. Starting at a side strut on the bottom ring, turn in the raw edge of the fabric the width of one pleat and pin in position at the top and bottom rings, leaving 1.3 cm (½ in.) fabric extending beyond the bottom ring (fig. 291). Make sure that the grain of the fabric is in line with the fold of the pleat.

154

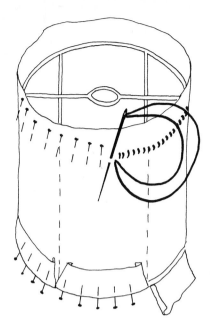

Fig. 290 Slashing lining at bottom ring, making turnings of 0.6 cm (¼ in.) on each side edge

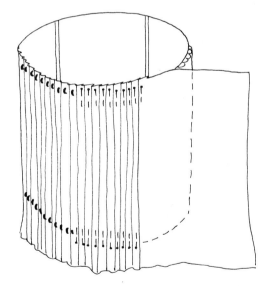

Fig. 291 Pleating pinned and stitched into position at top and bottom rings

(c)   Pleat and pin the fabric along the bottom ring until the next strut is reached, making sure that the 1.3 cm (½ in.) overlap at the bottom ring is kept

perfectly straight, and that the fold lines of each pleat are in line with the grain of the fabric.

(d)   At the completion of one section, draw up the pleats to the top ring and pin into position (fig. 291). Oversew pleating at the top and bottom rings.

(e)   Continue pleating in this way, pleating, pinning and sewing one section at a time, until the last strut is reached. Make sure the same number of pleats is worked in each section. To finish off the pleating slip the end of the last pleat underneath the very first pleat and complete the stitching.

(f)   To join the strips of fabric together simply overlap at the end of the first set of pleating to form another pleat. No seaming is necessary.

(g)   To neaten the lining at the top ring trim the fabric back to the stitching and fold the lining over the pleating. Stitch back as in fig. 292, using one large and one small oversewing stitch and a single thread. Neaten the bottom edge by turning the fabric back and sewing in the same way. Trim off to the stitching.

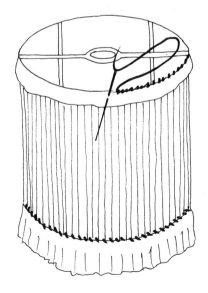

Fig. 292 Neatening lining at top ring

155

(h) Apply trimming as explained on page 149. This method can also be used for straight-sided empire and cone shapes, but when using these it is advisable to have a space between each pleat on the bottom ring to allow for the overlap of the pleating at the smaller top ring. The same number of pleats have to be fitted into a smaller space and so the size of the space at the bottom ring must be adjusted to suit the individual lampshade (fig. 293).

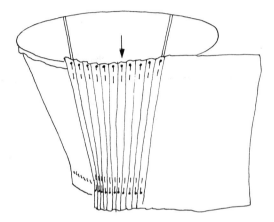

Fig. 293 **Straight-sided empire showing equal space and equal pleat at bottom ring and the correct positioning of the centre pleat**

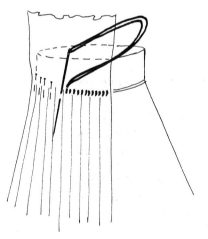

Fig. 294 **Pleating pinned and stitched to lower ring of collar**

When making a pleated lampshade with a collar, the pleating is pinned and sewn to the lower ring of the collar before being pleated up to the top ring (fig. 294).

Fan-pleated lampshade

This is worked in exactly the same way as straight pleating, following the same basic principles. Care must be taken, however, to measure and mark out the arrangement for each set of pleats on the top and bottom rings before the work is started. Use a straight-sided frame for this type of pleating.

Small sets of pleats should be made alternately at the top and bottom rings, and then drawn up and stitched in the usual way. A separate piece of fabric is used for each set of pleats, and this is very effective if worked in two colours of chiffon, or in two shades of one colour (figs. 295 and 296). The size of each set of pleats is governed by the design and size of the frame.

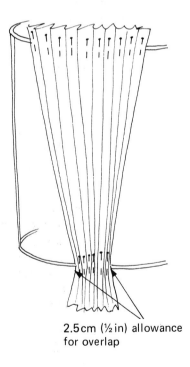

2.5 cm (½ in) allowance
for overlap

Fig. 295 **First set of fan pleating pinned in position showing an allowance of 2.5 cm (½ in.) at each side of the pleating**

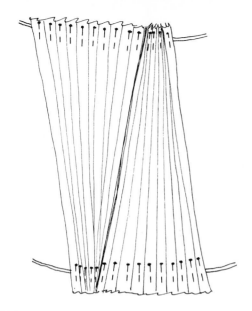

Fig. 296 **Second set of fan pleating pinned in position**

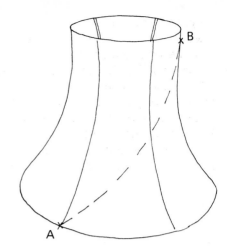

Fig. 297 **Measuring for a swathed pleated lampshade**

Swathed pleated lampshade
Swathed pleated lampshades are more difficult to make successfully than straight pleated ones, but with a little care and patience a good result can be achieved. Try making a straight pleated one first to gain experience with pleating.

(a)   Use a curved empire frame for this type of lampshade.
(b)   Prepare and tape the frame.
(c)   To estimate the amount of fabric, measure the circumference of the bottom ring and multiply by three to obtain the width, then measure the lampshade with a tape measure from the bottom of the first strut A and up and across to the top ring B, missing out one strut (fig. 297) to obtain the depth. Add 5 cm (2 in.) to this measurement.
(d)   Prepare and apply the lining as for the straight pleated shade.
(e)   Prepare the chiffon by tearing or cutting it into strips of the required depth and cutting off the selvedges.
(f)   Pin the first pleat in position folding in the raw edge. Pleat and pin the fabric

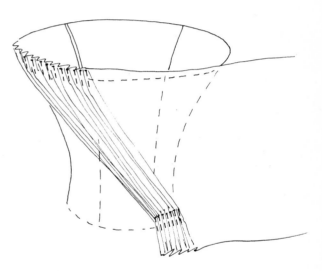

Fig. 298 **Pleating pinned in position, showing 1.3 cm (½ in.) overlap at bottom ring**

onto the bottom ring until one section of the frame has been completed(fig. 298). Leave an equal space between each pleat and keep the fold of the pleat in line with the grain of the fabric, keeping a 1.3 cm (½ in.) overlap along the bottom ring.

(g)   To drape the fabric to the top ring, take the first pleat and drape up and across to the top ring, stretching the fabric gently.

157

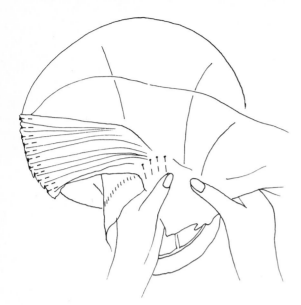

Fig. 299 **Swathing the pleating to the top ring missing out one strut**

Miss the next strut and pin to the following one. Drape each pleat in turn. There must be the same number of pleats at the top ring as at the bottom ring, but as the same amount of material has to be fitted into the top section, the pleats at the top will be much smaller and will overlap considerably (fig. 299).

(h) When one section has been completed satisfactorily adjust the pins at the top and bottom rings to make sure the pleats are taut and flat.

(i) Oversew this section at the top and bottom ring leaving only the first pleat pinned, so that the last pleat can be tucked underneath at the end.

(j) Continue pleating and draping each section in turn, checking that each has the same number of pleats. At the last strut, trim off fabric and tuck under the first pleat. Finish stitching. Neaten the top and bottom rings as before and apply the trimming.

Sunray-pleated lampshade

Several styles of frame are suitable for this type of pleating, as only one or two of the sections or panels are treated in this way.

(a) Prepare and tape the frame.

(b) To estimate the amount of fabric required for the pleated section, measure round the section of the frame to be pleated and allow twice that measurement to obtain the width. Measure from the position of the motif to the bottom ring at its widest point (A B) and add 5 cm (2 in.) to obtain the depth (fig. 300).

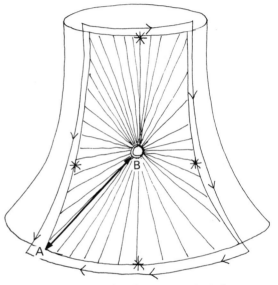

Fig. 300 **Measuring for fabric required for sunray pleating; section marked into four equal parts**

(c) Two linings are necessary for this style of shade; one is used as an interlining and is applied as for an external lining (fig. 290), and the other is used for a balloon lining and is applied after the cover had been completed (fig. 272). Prepare these linings as on page 141.

(d) Apply and sew the interlining into position and mark the position for the motif.

(e) Measure and mark out the section to be pleated into four equal parts.

(f) Cut the fabric to be pleated into strips the depth and width required. Make two rows of gathering stitches along one of the long sides 0.6 cm (¼ in.) from the raw edge. If necessary, join the strips

158

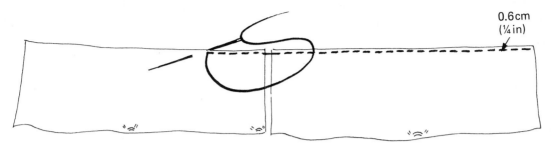

0.6cm
(¼in)

Fig. 301 **Strip of fabric marked with tailor tacks into four equal sections**

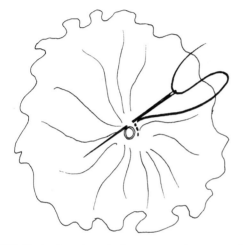

Fig. 302 **Gathering threads drawn up and sewn to the centre of the section**

together with the gathering stitches. With tailor tacks mark off the strip of fabric into four equal sections (fig. 301). Draw up the gathering threads tightly into a small circle and sew firmly to the interlining at the centre of the section (fig. 302).

(g) Pin the outer edges of the circle of fabric to the frame, matching guide marks and tailor tacks (fig. 303). Space the pleats evenly round the section. Oversew into position and trim off to the stitching. Apply the motif firmly to the gathered raw edge in the centre (fig. 304).

(h) Insert the balloon lining as on page 146.

(i) Apply crossway strip to neaten the stitches on the struts and apply trimmings to the top and bottom rings.

FIRM LAMPSHADES

Firm lampshades are quick and easy to make, but by combining other crafts and skills, unusual and original ideas can be achieved. For example, dried flowers and grasses can be introduced, or appliqué, fabric printing or oil painting. Lacemaking, macrame and crochet and many forms of embroidery can all be used to great advantage.

Materials
Buckram
This is a stiff cloth with a coarse rough weave which gives an interesting texture.

Fig. 303 **Pleating and pinning the outer edges of the circle of fabric to the frame**

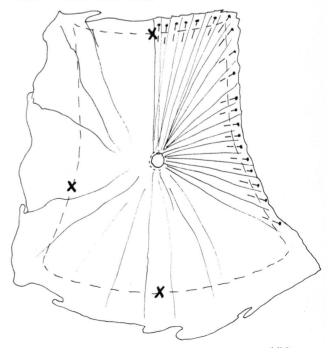

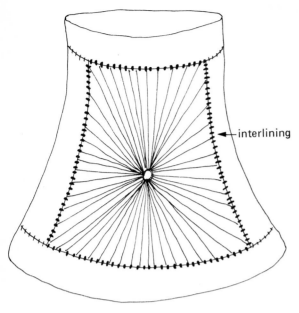

Fig. 304 **Central motif applied to lampshade**

It can be tinted or dyed and is a useful foundation for delicate fabrics such as lace or embroidery. It can also be used for backing appliqué, dried flowers and grasses and other decorative materials.

To use buckram, wipe over the smooth side with a damp sponge before ironing on the fabric with a hot iron. Cover the fabric with a damp cloth and press again. Motifs of lace or embroidery can be applied to buckram using this method and if necessary a little adhesive can be used.

Pelmet buckram
This is also a useful fabric, as its golden brown surface has an interesting texture.

Covered lampshade card
This can be obtained at many department stores and craft shops and is ready to use. Fabric is bonded onto the card, but the range available is rather limited.

Iron-on lampshade parchment
This is available at craft shops and department stores and is a parchment with an adhesive on one side. Light to medium weight fabrics can be successfully applied to this. The fabric is placed onto the adhesive side and ironed

on with a hot iron. The heat releases the adhesive and the fabric sticks firmly to the surface. If using delicate fabrics test a small piece first to make sure it will withstand a hot iron.

Parchment
Real parchment in the form of old maps and deeds can be used provided it is not stained and wrinkled.

Most firm shades cannot be washed because of their paper content, so they should be kept clean by regular brushing with a soft brush.

Straight-sided drum lampshade
Two rings of exactly the same size are used for making this type of shade (see fig. 260). One should be plain and the other should have a fitting attached, e.g. a gimbal or a pendant. About twelve wooden clothes pegs with springs are required to hold the fabric to the rings or frame.

(a) Prepare and tape the rings as on page 141.
(b) To estimate the amount of material required, measure round the taped rings to find the circumference of the shade, then decide on the height of the finished lampshade.
(c) Make a pattern using stiff paper, cutting it into a rectangle the required depth (height of shade) and width (circumference of shade) plus 1.3 cm (½ in.) for a seam allowance.
(d) Fit the pattern onto the rings using the wooden clothes pegs, and check the proportion of the shade and the fit of the pattern, adjusting if necessary.
(e) Cut out the fabric very carefully using the paper pattern and attach to the rings using the wooden clothes pegs (fig. 305).
(f) With a double thread and a strong needle (Betweens 5/6) sew through the fabric to the tape round the top and bottom rings, using a blanket stitch (fig. 305). These stitches are covered by the trimming. Make sure that the fabric does not extend above or below the rings or it will give an ugly appearance to the finished shade.

(g) Finish sewing 5 cm (2 in.) from where the seam is to be positioned (usually at the side of the shade). Mark a seam allowance of 0.6 cm (¼ in.) using a ruler and pencil on the wrong side of the fabric and trim off the excess fabric using a sharp pair of scissors to ensure a perfectly even edge (fig. 306).

(h) Overlap the seam and apply adhesive evenly to both edges. Press together firmly until the seam is secure. Finish blanket stitching at the top and bottom rings.

(i) Apply the trimming with an adhesive. Turn in the ends 0.6 cm (¼ in.) and butt together.

Fig. 306 **Cutting line for seam**

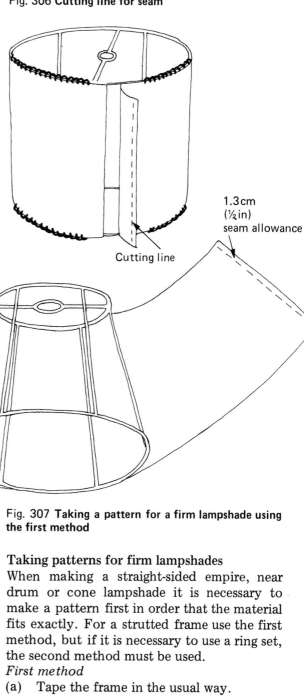

1.3cm
(½in)
seam allowance

Cutting line

Fig. 307 **Taking a pattern for a firm lampshade using the first method**

Taking patterns for firm lampshades

When making a straight-sided empire, near drum or cone lampshade it is necessary to make a pattern first in order that the material fits exactly. For a strutted frame use the first method, but if it is necessary to use a ring set, the second method must be used.

First method

(a) Tape the frame in the usual way.

◄ Fig. 305 **Fabric in position using wooden clothes pegs, and sewn in place using blanket stitch**

(b) Take a large piece of stiff paper and place the taped frame onto this, holding it firmly.

(c) Starting at the side strut, mark along the outside of the strut with a pencil and mark the top and bottom. Rotate the frame slowly marking along the top and bottom rings until the first strut is reached. Allow 1.3 cm (½ in.) seam allowance at one end (fig. 307). Make sure the frame is held firmly or an accurate pattern will not be obtained.

(d) If a large frame is being used the pattern can be taken from one half of the frame only. Two pieces of fabric can then be cut out from the same pattern, but remember to reverse the pattern when cutting out the fabric for the second half.

(e) Cut out the pattern, fit onto the frame and adjust if necessary.

Second method

(a) Make this pattern using graph paper (figs. 308 and 309).

(b) Tape the rings, and take the following measurements: the required height of the shade, the diameter and circumference of the top ring, and the diameter and circumference of the bottom ring.

(c) On the graph paper, draw a horizontal line CD, which is the diameter of the bottom ring. At the middle of CD, which is X, draw a vertical line from X to Y. This equals the required height of

Fig. 308 **Taking measurements requried to make a pattern for a cone lampshade using the second method**

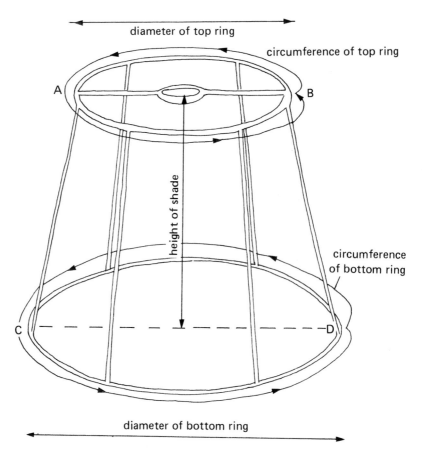

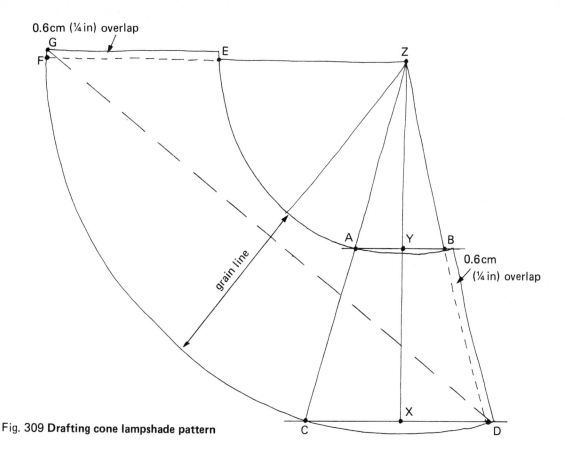

0.6cm (¼ in) overlap

grain line

0.6cm (¼ in) overlap

Fig. 309 **Drafting cone lampshade pattern**

the shade. Angle YXD is a right angle of 90 degrees.

(d) Draw a horizontal line through Y making it parallel with CD. AB equals the diameter of the top ring, with AY equal to YB.

(e) Join CA and DB, and continue these lines until they meet the perpendicular line at Z. If the pattern is accurate the two lines meet at the same point.

(f) With a large compass, using Z as the centre, draw two arcs of circles: the first with radius ZB and the second with radius ZD. If a compass is not available use a piece of buckram with a drawing pin in one end at Z. Make a hole in the buckram at the correct point and push a pencil point through it.

(g) First draw the arc from point B round to

point E (this is the circumference of the top ring) then draw an arc from point D to point F (this is the circumference of the bottom ring). This gives the size of the shade. Add 0.6 cm (¼ in.) for an overlapping join in the shade.

(h) Join FE and continue the line. This should pass through point Z if the pattern is accurate.

(i) Place a ruler between D and G and mark the centre. From this point place the ruler to Z and mark a grain line.

(j) Cut out the pattern and try on the rings. When an accurate pattern has been obtained and the fit is satisfactory, cut out the lampshade fabric using the pattern and noting the grain line.

(k) Make up the shade using the method for the straight sided shade (see page 160).

163

Suppliers

John Lewis & Co Ltd
Oxford St
London W1 (and branches)
Shower curtain fabric; furnishing fabrics; roller blind kits and fabrics; lampshade frames, fabrics and trimmings; patchwork templates; downproof cambric

Distinctive Trimmings & Co Ltd
11 Marylebone Lane
London W1
and
17 Church St
London W8
Trimmings for lampshades and soft furnishings

Rufflette Ltd
59 St James's St
London SW1
Curtain heading tapes and accessories; decorative braids and trimmings; tracks and poles

Russell Trading Co
75 Paradise St
Liverpool L1 38P
Soft furnishing fabrics; down and feather and synthetic fillings; transfers for English quilting; lampshade fabrics; postal service; catalogue available

Beckford Mill
Harden
Bingley
W. Yorkshire
Synthetic fillings; pads for quilts; postal service; catalogue available

Limericks (Linens) Ltd
110 Court Rd
Westcliffe-on-sea
Essex
Down; downproof cambric; cushion pads; sheeting; postal service; catalogue available

Kirsch (Antiference) Ltd
Curtain heading tapes and accessories; tracks and poles

A. M. Row & Son Ltd
42 Market Place
Ripon
Yorkshire
Patchwork templates

A Sanderson & Son Ltd
Berners St
London W1
Soft furnishing fabrics

The Lampshade Supply Service
21 Jerdan Place
London SW6
Lampshade frames made to order

F. Barrett & Son
51-53 Christchurch Rd
Ringwood
Hants
Soft furnishing fabrics; lampshade frames and fabrics

Habitat shops
Roller blind kits and fabric

Fred Aldous Ltd
The Handicraft Centre
PO Box 135
37 Lever St
Manchester M50 1UX
Lampshade frames, fabrics, trimmings

Nottingham Handicrafts Co
(School Suppliers)
Melton Rd
West Bridgford
Nottingham NG2 6HD
Lampshade frames, fabrics, trimmings

Glossary

British terms and their American equivalents

airing cupboard—airing closet where linens are dried
bump—coarse fabric or matting
calico—unbleached muslin
cambric—closely woven, polished cotton
card—cardboard
crossway strip—bias strip cut from fabric
cushions—all decorative pillows other than bed pillows
domette—baize or coarse flannel in which the warp is cotton and the filling woollen
duvet—bed covering used in Northern Europe that takes the place of both top sheet and blankets
electric points—electrical outlets

hessian—coarse sacking; burlap
loose cover—slipcover
meter stick—yardstick
pelmet—fixture at head of curtains that conceals rod and fittings
perspex—lucite
repp—transversely corded or ribbed fabric
roller blinds—window shades
set square—right triangle, usually used with T square
tacking cotton—basting thread
Terylene—Dacron
turnings—seam allowance
Vilene—stiff bonded fabric used for interfacing
wadding—batting or filling
window treatments—window furnishings
zip—zipper

Bibliography

Textiles
Textiles: Properties and Behaviour, Edward Miller (Batsford 1973)
Fibres and Fabrics of Today, Helen Thompson (Heinemann 3rd ed 1974) (The Horn Book, Boston, 1974)
Fabrics for Interiors, J Larsen and J Weeks (Van Nostrand Reinhold, New York, 1975)
The Butterick Fabric Handbook : A Consumer's Guide to Fabrics for Clothing and Home Furnishings, Irene Kleeberg (Butterick, New York, 1975)

Needlework
The Anchor Manual of Needlework, J & P Coats (Batsford 1958) (Branford, Boston, 1958)
Machine Stitches, Anne Butler (Batsford 1976)
Embroidery Stitches, Barbara Snook (Batsford 1975) (Crown, New York, 1975)
Cross Stitch Patterns, Irmgard Gierl (Batsford 1977) (Scribner, New York, 1977)
Dictionary of Stitches, Mary Thomas (Hodder & Stoughton 1965)
Designs for Machine Embroidery, Ira Lillow (Batsford 1975) (Branford, Boston, 1975)
Embroidery from Traditional English Patterns, Ruby Evans (Batsford 1971)
Patchwork, Averil Colby (Batsford 1976) (Branford, Boston, 1976)
Patchwork Quilts, Averil Colby (Batsford 1965) (Scribner, New York, 1975)
Quilting, Averil Colby (Batsford 1972) (Scribner, New York, 1972)
Simple Patchwork, Alice Timmins (Batsford 1973)
Patchwork Simplified, Alice Timmins (Arco, New York, 1973)
Patterns for Patchwork Quilts and Cushions, Susy Ives (Batsford 1977)
The Patchwork Point of View, Jill Jarnow (Simon & Schuster, 1975)
Step-by-Step Quiltmaking, Barbara Danneman (Western Publishing, New York, 1975)
Quilting, Patchwork, Appliqué, Trapunto, Thelma Newman (Crown, New York, 1974)

Home crafts
Lampshades: Technique and Design, Angela Fishburn (Batsford 1975) (Drake, New York, 1977)
Making Plaits and Braids, June Barker (Batsford 1973) (Branford, Boston, 1973)
Introducing Macramé, Eirian Short (Batsford 1970)
Fabric Furnishings, Margaret Butler and Beryl Greves (Batsford 1972) (Drake, New York, 1972)
Making Loose Covers, Donald R Porter (Batsford 1975)
Upholstering, Malcolm Flitman (Batsford 1972) (Drake, New York, 1972)
Upholstery Repair and Restoration, Robert J McDonald (Batsford 1977) (Scribner, New York, 1977)
Make Your Own Rugs, Dietrich Kirsch and Jutta Kirsch-Korn (Batsford 1970)
Sewing for Your Home, Better Homes & Gardens (Meredith, Des Moines, Iowa, 1974)

Index